FIXING AUSTRALIAN POLITICS

HOW TO CHANGE THE SYSTEM OF GOVERNMENT

EDDY JOKOVICH + DAVID LEWIS

NP
NEW POLITICS

Fixing Australian Politics: How to change the system of government
ISBN (paperback): 978-1-7635701-0-8
ISBN (Amazon):   979-8-3249179-2-0

May 2024. Published by New Politics, an imprint of ARMEDIA Pty. Ltd.

New Politics
PO Box 1265, Darlinghurst NSW 1300
www.newpolitics.com.au
Email: info@newpolitics.com.au

Production: ARMEDIA

Published and produced on the lands of the Wangal and Whadjuk people.

EDITORIAL NOTE ON THE USE OF AI TECHNOLOGY
We employ artificial intelligence tools in the editing process of our articles.
These tools assisted with transcriptions of audio recordings, grammar
correction, refinement and formatting.

A catalogue record for this
work is available from the
National Library of Australia

NATIONAL
LIBRARY
OF AUSTRALIA

CONTENTS

CHAPTER 6: CONSTITUTIONAL REFORM

CHAPTER 7: REPRESENTATION AND DIVERSITY

EPILOGUE: FIXING AUSTRALIAN POLITICS

ABOUT THE EDITORS

A VISION FOR REFORMING AUSTRALIAN POLITICS

INTRODUCTION

Australia's political landscape stands on the precipice of transformation. The need for comprehensive reform is palpable, driven by evolving societal values, demands for greater transparency, and a push towards inclusivity. *Fixing Australian Politics: How to change the system of government* outlines a multifaceted strategy to reshape Australian politics across various fronts—electoral systems, campaign finance, governance, media interaction, constitutional matters, and diversity in representation.

Many of the ideas presented in *Fixing Australian Politics* have been key discussion points in over 200 episodes of the New Politics podcast, as well as in many of our writings about these matters. It is crucial to document and consolidate these ideas into a single framework—this is the primary reason for why we have created this book. This will facilitate future debates and discussions, which can then provide governments and policymakers with a clear and concise pathway for improving governance in Australia.

We begin with electoral reform, advocating for the introduction of proportional representation to ensure that every vote contributes equally to the political outcome, mirroring a more democratic representation in parliament. Maintaining mandatory voting also remains crucial to preserving high voter turnout and ensuring that electoral results reflect the true will of the people. In addition, we also recommend the shift towards implementing online voting systems to modernise the voting process, making it more accessible and efficient while upholding the integrity of each vote.

Financial influences in politics demand urgent restructuring and this is an issue that had dogged Australian political affairs for far too long. The proposal for full public funding of elections seeks to curb the undue influence of wealthy donors and level the playing field for all candidates, and reducing donation caps and managing political donations in the public interest are steps designed to enhance the transparency of financial contributions and prevent corruption.

Further reforms are necessary to fortify the mechanisms that ensure politicians and public officials are held accountable. While the implementation of the National Corruption Against Corruption in 2023 was a belated and much needed reform, there needs to be tighter corruption measures, improved Freedom of Information legislation, and enhanced protection for whistleblowers and public informants to provide an environment of transparency and trust in government operations.

The governance of political parties also requires recalibration. Introducing term limits would prevent the entrenchment of power, encouraging fresh ideas and perspectives in leadership. Strengthening parliamentary committees and reforming Question Time to become a more effective tool for scrutinising government actions, rather than the current structure where the government of the day uses it to deflect, score political points and humiliate the opposition, are also critical for increasing accountability and enhancing the legislative process.

In an era of misinformation and disinformation, it is crucial to reinforce financial support for public media and advocate for truth in journalism to maintain an informed electorate. This effort should be accompanied by a reformed and more powerful Australian Press Council, which currently resembles a toothless tiger and often succumbs to the interests of mainstream media. Public media must be empowered to operate independently from government influence, providing balanced and comprehensive coverage of national affairs.

The call for a new Australian Constitution underscores the necessity to mirror contemporary values and the multicultural identity of the nation. The current Constitution, developed in the 1890s and implemented in 1901, was designed to unify the Australian colonies. However, this unification was inherently limited: Indigenous Australians and women were excluded from the constitutional conventions that led to federation. It was crafted by white men adorned with long beards, moustaches, and top hats— how can such a document remain relevant over 120 years later? Also, this Constitution has proven almost unchangeable, like an albatross around the nation's neck. Out of 45 referendums aimed at modernising the Constitution to make it more relevant, only eight have been successful. This is a situation that is unsustainable. Recognising Indigenous Australians and their unique rights, alongside implementing an Australian republic, are also crucial steps toward honouring the country's heritage and redefining its identity on the global stage.

Ensuring broader engagement in politics involves implementing quotas for underrepresented groups and improving youth engagement—lowering the voting age to 16 would be an excellent start—as would a range of issues to address the general disinterest in politics and strengthening civic education to cultivate a more politically aware and active citizenry.

We recognise that expecting all these changes to happen quickly is naïve. Over a quarter of a century has passed since the referendum on the republic was held and defeated in 1999, and today, the issue barely rates a mention in public discourse. Political reform in Australia is hampered by the structures and barriers of its own institutionalised system, and any change—if it occurs at all—moves at a glacial pace.

The Liberal–National Coalition refuses to consider any change at all and ramps up fear campaigns as a stalling tactic; while the Labor Party fears the changes that it should be advocated for, anxious it might offend the vested business and media interests who benefit most from the status quo. Change of any nature takes time, but initially, there must be political will. For far too long, Australia has lacked this essential ingredient for change.

This sweeping array of reforms contained in *Fixing Australian Politics* presents a bold blueprint for the future of Australian politics. By addressing these key areas, the aim is to create a more robust, inclusive, and transparent political system that is equipped to meet the challenges of the twenty-first century and reflect the diverse voices of all Australians, each of which is critical for the rejuvenation of the nation's political framework and the restoration of public faith in the democratic process.

*

CHAPTER 1: ELECTORAL REFORM

INTRODUCE PROPORTIONAL REPRESENTATION

The proposal to introduce proportional representation into Australia's electoral system seeks to ensure a more accurate and fair representation of voters' preferences in the legislature. By allocating seats in proportion to the percentage of votes each party receives, proportional representation aims to address the limitations of the current preferential voting system, including the potential for disproportionate representation. While promising a more reflective and diverse political landscape, the transition to proportional representation would also bring challenges, including the need for significant changes to electoral processes and voter education. The potential benefits of increased fairness and diversity in representation make this proposal a compelling option for electoral reform in Australia.

Australia's electoral framework, with its roots deeply embedded in the tradition of preferential voting, stands as a distinctive feature that sets it apart in the democratic world. This system, fundamental to the way Australians engage with their democracy, mandates voters to rank candidates in order of preference. It's a method that was designed with the intention of ensuring that elected representatives gain office not merely by securing a plurality of votes but by achieving a majority through the redistribution of preferences from less popular candidates.

The intricacies of this system offer a more nuanced approach to democracy. It allows for a more representative form of election, ensuring that if a voter's primary choice doesn't have sufficient support to win, their vote can still contribute to the selection of a representative through their subsequent preferences. This method encourages a broader, more inclusive political conversation and can lead to more moderate, centrist policies, as candidates seek to appeal not only to their direct supporters but also to be the preferable secondary choice of others.

However, the preferential voting system is not without its criticisms and complexities. One significant issue is the potential for a discrepancy between the percentage of votes a party receives and the number of seats it wins in the legislature. In certain instances, this can lead to a party receiving a major portion of the first-preference votes but not securing a corresponding proportion of legislative seats, especially if their support is concentrated in a few areas or is too spread out to be the majority in any. Conversely, parties with lower overall first-preference votes can achieve better representation if their candidates are frequently ranked as a second or third preference. This outcome is reflective of the system's design to mirror voter preferences more accurately, but it can also lead to debates about the fairness and representativeness of the electoral outcomes.

Despite such debates, the preferential voting system is deeply ingrained in Australia's political fabric, which was first established in 1918, after the *Electoral Act* was comprehensively rewritten. It requires voters to engage more fully with the electoral process, demanding a greater understanding of the candidates and parties on offer. This engagement can be seen as a double-edged sword: on one hand, it fosters a more informed electorate that considers the full spectrum of options; on the other hand, it places a higher cognitive demand on voters, which could potentially disenfranchise those less willing or able to navigate the complexities of the system.

The system also impacts the political landscape, encouraging a multi-party system and the formation of coalitions, as no single party is likely to dominate the preference flow entirely. This aspect of the voting system fosters negotiation and compromise among political entities, traits that are essential in a healthy democracy.

TRANSITIONING TO PROPORTIONAL REPRESENTATION

In the evolving landscape of Australian politics, a significant proposal has been put forth to transition the electoral system to proportional representation. This proposed shift is aimed at addressing some of the inherent limitations of the current preferential voting system by ensuring that the allocation of seats in the legislature more accurately mirrors the distribution of votes among the parties. The essence of proportional representation is straightforward yet profound: it seeks to establish a direct correlation between the percentage of votes a party receives and the percentage of seats it occupies in the legislature, thereby promising a more equitable and representative form of governance.

This shift towards proportional representation is motivated by a desire to enhance the fairness of the electoral process. Advocates argue that under the current system, it's possible for parties to secure a significant share of seats with only a marginal lead in the popular vote, or conversely, for parties to receive a sizable portion of the vote without a corresponding representation in the legislature. Such discrepancies can lead to questions about the legitimacy of the electoral outcomes and the extent to which the parliament truly reflects the will of the people.

The move to proportional representation is seen as a remedy to these concerns, offering a system that is inherently designed to match the popular vote with legislative representation. In doing so, it acknowledges the diversity of political opinion within the electorate and ensures that minority voices are heard and represented in the political arena. This inclusivity not only enriches the democratic process but also encourages greater participation, as voters see a direct link between their vote and its impact on the political landscape.

Proportional representation could lead to a more pluralistic political environment, where smaller parties and independent candidates have a genuine chance of gaining representation. This could encourage a wider range of viewpoints in policy debates and decision-making processes, fostering a more vibrant and dynamic political discourse. In a proportional representation system, coalition governments become more likely, requiring parties to engage in dialogue and compromise. While some might view the prospect of coalition governance with caution, fearing instability or indecisiveness, others see it as an opportunity for more collaborative and consensus-driven politics.

However, the transition to proportional representation is not without its challenges. Implementing such a system requires careful consideration of the method used to allocate seats proportionally, whether through party lists, single transferable votes, or another mechanism. Each of these methods has its nuances and implications for how political campaigns are conducted, how parties prioritise candidates, and how voters engage with the electoral process. There's a need to ensure that the system remains accessible and understandable to the electorate, to maintain or even enhance the current levels of voter engagement and trust in the electoral process.

The proposal to introduce proportional representation into the Australian electoral system is, at its core, an attempt to refine the country's democracy, making it more reflective of and responsive to the diverse views within its society.

THE BENEFITS OF PROPORTIONAL REPRESENTATION

One of the most compelling advantages of proportional representation is its potential to foster a more diverse and inclusive political environment. Traditional voting systems often marginalise smaller parties and independent candidates, making it difficult for them to gain a foothold in the legislative process despite having substantial public support. Proportional representation disrupts this status quo by ensuring that these groups have a fair chance at representation, thereby enriching the political discourse with a wider array of perspectives. This inclusivity is crucial in a multicultural society, where diverse viewpoints and interests must find expression and advocacy within the political system. By bringing these voices into the legislative arena, proportional representation strengthens the democratic process, making it more representative of society's multifaceted nature.

The adoption of proportional representation can significantly reduce the phenomenon of wasted votes, a common critique of winner-takes-all systems where votes for losing candidates or those that exceed the threshold for winning are effectively disregarded. Under proportional representation, nearly every vote plays a role in determining the composition of the legislature, thereby enhancing the value of each vote and potentially increasing voter engagement. Voters are more likely to participate in the electoral process when they feel their vote has the power to effect change, even if their preferred candidate or party does not have a majority. This increased engagement is fundamental to the health and vitality of a democracy, as it reflects a populace that is actively involved in shaping its governance.

The benefits of proportional representation extend beyond the mechanics of voting and representation to influence the political culture of a nation. By encouraging the formation of coalitions, proportional representation necessitates dialogue, negotiation, and compromise among political parties. This collaborative approach to governance can lead to more balanced and considerate policy-making, as legislation must garner support from a broader spectrum of the political landscape. The presence of a more varied group of representatives in the legislature acts as a check against the dominance of any single party, promoting a more equitable distribution of power and fostering accountability.

The shift towards a proportional representation system could have a stabilising effect on the political environment. When parties recognise that their chances of representation are directly tied to their share of the popular vote, there is an incentive to engage more constructively with the electorate and to pursue policies that have broad appeal. This can lead to a political climate that prioritises long-term strategy and policy development over short-term electoral gains, contributing to more sustainable governance.

CHALLENGES AND CONSIDERATIONS OF PROPORTIONAL REPRESENTATION

The adoption of proportional representation in Australia—or in any democracy—encompasses not only its potential benefits but also the significant challenges and considerations that accompany such a transformative change. The implementation of proportional representation involves a comprehensive overhaul of the electoral system, which carries implications for the political landscape, the operation of political parties, and the engagement of voters with the democratic process.

One of the foremost challenges lies in the implementation process itself. Transitioning to a proportional representation system necessitates wide-ranging modifications to existing electoral laws and processes. This might include the redesign of electoral districts to accommodate multi-member constituencies, a hallmark of many proportional representation systems, which itself raises questions about how best to ensure equitable representation across diverse geographic and demographic communities. The development of new voting and counting methods to accurately capture and reflect voters' preferences in a proportional manner would also be required. This technical and logistical undertaking would demand significant resources, expertise, and time, highlighting the need for careful planning and management to ensure a smooth transition.

Another critical consideration is the impact of proportional representation on the political landscape. By facilitating a more equitable representation of small parties, proportional representation could significantly alter the balance of power within the legislature. While this shift towards a more inclusive and representative political arena is a driving force behind the push for proportional representation, it also poses challenges for governance and stability. The likely increase in the number of parties represented in parliament could necessitate the formation of coalition governments, which, although common in many democracies with proportional representation, require a different set of skills and a greater emphasis on compromise and negotiation. This could lead to a more complex and dynamic political environment, with potential implications for policy continuity and legislative productivity.

The introduction of proportional representation also brings to the fore the critical issue of voter education. A change in the electoral system is not merely a procedural adjustment but a fundamental shift in how representation is achieved and understood. Voters would need to be thoroughly educated on the mechanics of the new system, including how to cast their votes and the implications of their choices. Understanding the nuances of proportional representation, such as the significance of party lists, the role of thresholds for representation, and the mechanism for translating votes into seats, is essential for voters to effectively participate in the democratic process. This educational endeavour is monumental, requiring concerted efforts from government bodies, civil society, and the media to ensure that the electorate is well-informed and confident in their engagement with the new system.

These challenges and considerations underscore the complexity of transitioning to a proportional representation system. Implementation demands careful thought, robust planning, and a willingness to navigate the uncertainties inherent in such a significant change. The impact on the political landscape, while offering the promise of a more representative and inclusive democracy, also necessitates adjustments in political strategy, governance approaches, and voter engagement. Meanwhile, the imperative of voter education highlights the need for a comprehensive and inclusive approach to informing the electorate, ensuring that every voter is empowered to participate fully and effectively in the new system.

MAINTAIN MANDATORY VOTING

Mandatory voting enforcement is advocated as a means to bolster democratic participation and ensure that election results more accurately represent the will of the entire electorate. By requiring all eligible citizens to vote, this approach aims to increase turnout, reduce socio-economic disparities in participation, and enhance the legitimacy of the democratic process. However, the enforcement of mandatory voting also raises concerns regarding individual freedoms, the practical challenges of implementation, and the potential impact on the quality of voter engagement. Balancing these factors is crucial in assessing the viability and desirability of mandatory voting as a policy to strengthen democracy.

THE PRINCIPLE OF MANDATORY VOTING

The principle of mandatory voting introduces a distinctive dimension to the democratic fabric of a nation, setting forth a compelling narrative on the civic duties and responsibilities of its citizens. At the heart of mandatory voting laws lies the directive that all eligible citizens must partake in the electoral process, an obligation that can manifest as casting a vote or merely presenting oneself at a polling station on election day, subject to the nuances of the legal framework governing such mandates.

This principle is underpinned by the notion that democratic governance is not only a right but also a responsibility shared by all members of society. By compelling participation, mandatory voting seeks to reinforce the foundational premise of democracy—that the legitimacy and efficacy of governmental authority derive from the consent and active involvement of the governed. This ethos positions voting not just as a personal choice but as a civic duty, integral to the maintenance and vitality of democratic institutions.

Mandatory voting addresses several critical challenges facing democracies today, including voter apathy, low turnout, and the disproportionate influence of certain demographic groups over others in the political process. In societies where voting is optional, disparities in participation rates can lead to electoral outcomes that do not accurately reflect the diverse spectrum of views and needs within the populace. By ensuring that all segments of society are represented in the voting process, mandatory voting aims to produce more equitable and representative governance, diminishing the risk of disenfranchisement and marginalisation of minority voices.

The practice of mandatory voting can serve as a catalyst for greater political engagement and awareness among citizens. Knowing that participation is a requirement, individuals may be more inclined to educate themselves on the issues at stake and the positions of various candidates and parties. This heightened level of informed participation is conducive to a more vibrant and substantive democratic discourse, fostering a populace that is not only more attuned to the complexities of governance but also more adept at holding elected officials accountable.

However, the implementation of mandatory voting is not devoid of challenges and ethical considerations. Central to the debate is the balance between individual freedom and collective responsibility. Critics argue that compulsory participation infringes upon personal liberty, including the right to abstain as a form of political expression. The effectiveness of mandatory voting thus hinges on the careful design of the legal framework, ensuring that it respects individual freedoms while promoting the collective good. This includes provisions for conscientious objection and the implementation of nominal penalties for non-compliance, which serve as gentle reminders of civic obligations rather than punitive measures.

The success of mandatory voting in enhancing democratic participation and representation is contingent upon the broader context of electoral fairness and accessibility. Ensuring that all citizens have the means and opportunity to vote, through measures such as accessible polling locations, early voting, and voter education programs, is essential. Only in an environment that facilitates rather than obstructs participation can the principle of mandatory voting truly fulfill its democratic potential.

MAXIMISING VOTER TURNOUT AS A DEMOCRATIC PRINCIPLE

Maximising voter turnout at elections stands as a central democratic principle, aiming to cultivate an electoral environment where the voices of all constituents are heard and accounted for. This objective transcends mere numerical participation; it seeks to ensure that election outcomes embody a comprehensive and multifaceted portrayal of the electorate's preferences, bridging the gap between governance and the governed. At its core, this principle challenges the status quo of political engagement, aiming to extend beyond the traditionally active segments of society to include those who, whether due to apathy, disenfranchisement, or barriers to access, have historically been underrepresented in the democratic process.

The emphasis on maximising voter turnout is predicated on the belief that a democracy's legitimacy is bolstered by the breadth and depth of its electoral participation. Elections that capture a broad cross-section of society offer a more accurate reflection of public sentiment, lending credibility and authority to elected officials and the policies they enact. In contrast, when significant portions of the electorate abstain from voting—whether by choice or constraint— the resulting government may lack a full mandate, its policies not truly representative of the populace's diverse interests and needs.

Achieving high levels of voter turnout, therefore, is not merely a question of numbers but of inclusivity and equity. It involves dismantling barriers that hinder participation, whether they be physical, such as inaccessible polling locations; procedural, such as complicated registration processes; or societal, such as disillusionment with the political system. Efforts to enhance turnout must be multifaceted, addressing logistical, educational, and motivational aspects of voting. This includes making voting more accessible through early voting, mail-in ballots, and online options; simplifying the registration process; and conducting robust public education campaigns to inform voters about their rights and the importance of their participation.

Fostering a culture of voting where participation is viewed as both a right and a responsibility is also crucial. This involves not only institutional reforms but also societal shifts in how political engagement is perceived and valued. Encouraging discussions about politics and governance in diverse settings—from schools and workplaces to community centres and online forums—can help demystify the electoral process and highlight the tangible impact of political decisions on individuals' lives. By connecting the act of voting to the issues that matter most to people, the motivation to participate can be significantly enhanced.

Yet, the goal of maximising voter turnout also invites reflection on the deeper, structural challenges within democratic societies. Disillusionment or apathy towards voting often stems from a perception that the political system is unresponsive or that individual votes do not matter. Addressing these perceptions requires more than logistical fixes; it necessitates a commitment to political reform and responsiveness. Elected officials and political institutions must strive for transparency, accountability, and engagement with constituents, demonstrating that participation in the democratic process can lead to meaningful change.

The principle of maximising voter turnout is integral to the health and legitimacy of a democracy. It underscores the importance of every vote and the collective power of the electorate to shape its destiny. Achieving this objective demands a comprehensive approach that removes barriers to participation, educates and motivates voters, and fosters a political environment that values and responds to the voices of all citizens. In doing so, democracies can ensure that election outcomes truly reflect the will of the people, grounding governance in the broad and diverse spectrum of societal needs and aspirations.

THE BENEFITS OF MANDATORY VOTING

The institution of mandatory voting brings with it a suite of benefits that collectively contribute to the strengthening of democratic governance. By requiring all eligible citizens to participate in the electoral process, these laws act as a catalyst for higher voter turnout rates, making the act of voting more inclusive and emblematic of a democratic society's ideals. The advantages of such a system are manifold, touching on aspects of societal equity, representation, and the overall health of the democracy.

A paramount benefit of mandatory voting is the substantial increase in participation rates it typically ensures. This heightened turnout is not merely symbolic; it represents a more comprehensive engagement of the populace in the democratic process. When voter participation is maximised, the elected representatives emerge from a process that more accurately reflects the will of the entire electorate rather than a subset. This inclusivity bolsters the foundation of democratic governance, ensuring that decisions made reflect a broader consensus and are thus more representative of the society's collective will.

Mandatory voting plays a crucial role in reducing socio-economic disparities in voter turnout. In voluntary voting systems, it's well-documented that participation rates often correlate with certain socio-economic factors, including income, education, and employment status. This disparity can skew electoral outcomes towards the preferences of more privileged segments of society, leaving the needs and opinions of less privileged groups underrepresented. Mandatory voting mitigates this bias by leveling the playing field, compelling participation across all segments of society and thereby ensuring a more equitable representation. This inclusivity is crucial for the integrity of the democratic process, as it reaffirms the principle that every citizen, regardless of their socio-economic status, has an equal stake and an equal say in the governance of their society.

Another significant advantage of mandatory voting is the enhancement of political legitimacy. High voter turnout is often interpreted as a sign of a vibrant, healthy democracy. When electoral outcomes are determined by a majority of the populace, they carry a greater sense of legitimacy. This broad-based participation strengthens the mandate of elected officials and the policies they enact, as these are seen as more accurately reflecting the collective will. The sense of collective responsibility and involvement in the electoral process can also foster a deeper connection between citizens and their government, enhancing trust and confidence in the political system.

The benefits of mandatory voting extend beyond the immediate electoral process. By ensuring widespread participation, it encourages a more informed citizenry. Knowing that voting is compulsory, individuals may be more inclined to educate themselves on the issues at stake and the positions of different candidates or parties.

This informed engagement enriches the democratic dialogue and fosters a more substantive public discourse on policy matters. Additionally, mandatory voting can act as a counterbalance to the influence of money in politics. When every vote counts equally, the power of affluent groups to sway electoral outcomes through campaign financing is diluted, potentially leading to a more level playing field in political contests.

CHALLENGES AND CRITICISMS OF MANDATORY VOTING

While mandatory voting is advocated for its potential to enhance democratic participation and ensure a more representative electoral outcome, it is not without its challenges and criticisms. These concerns stem from considerations of individual freedom, the logistical hurdles of implementation and enforcement, and the impact on the quality of electoral participation.

One of the principal criticisms leveled against mandatory voting is that it infringes upon individual freedom of choice. In a democratic society, the right to vote is often viewed not just as a privilege or duty but as a personal freedom that includes the option to abstain. Critics argue that compelling individuals to vote under threat of penalty violates this fundamental democratic principle, constraining personal autonomy. From this perspective, the act of not voting can be seen as a valid form of political expression, reflecting dissatisfaction with the available candidates or the political system itself. Thus, mandatory voting, by obligating participation, may inadvertently undermine one of the very freedoms it seeks to bolster through increased electoral engagement.

The implementation and enforcement of mandatory voting laws also present significant challenges. To ensure compliance, a system must be in place to track whether citizens have voted and to administer penalties to those who fail to participate without a valid reason. This process requires a comprehensive and up-to-date voter registration system, effective mechanisms for monitoring turnout, and a judicious approach to penalising non-compliance. The complexity and cost of establishing and maintaining such a system can be substantial, raising questions about the efficient allocation of resources. The process of managing exemptions—for individuals unable to vote due to illness, disability, or other legitimate reasons—adds another layer of administrative complexity. Ensuring that these exemptions are applied fairly and consistently requires careful oversight, further complicating the enforcement of mandatory voting laws.

Another significant criticism concerns the quality versus the quantity of participation. The premise of mandatory voting is to increase electoral turnout, but some critics question whether simply boosting numbers leads to a more informed and engaged electorate. When participation is compulsory, it is possible that individuals who are otherwise disengaged or uninformed about the political process are forced to cast a vote. This could result in what some describe as "donkey votes"—randomly selected choices—or votes cast with minimal understanding of the candidates' platforms or policies.

The concern is that this might dilute the quality of electoral decisions, with outcomes based more on chance or superficial considerations than on a thoughtful assessment of the options. The challenge, then, is to ensure that measures to increase turnout also include efforts to enhance voter education and engagement, so that increased participation translates into a more informed electorate.

GLOBAL PERSPECTIVES ON MANDATORY VOTING

Mandatory voting is a fascinating study in global democratic diversity. Adopted by various countries around the world, this approach to electoral participation offers a range of different experiences, each reflecting unique historical, cultural, and political contexts. The global perspectives on mandatory voting, ranging from stringent enforcement to more symbolic implementation, illuminate the nuanced debate on its effectiveness and implications for democratic governance.

Countries such as Belgium, Australia, and Brazil represent some of the most notable examples of mandatory voting systems in action. Each of these nations has developed mechanisms to encourage compliance, from fines for non-participation in Belgium and Australia to the more severe implications of disenfranchisement from certain civil services in Brazil for those who fail to vote and do not provide a valid justification. These measures reflect a strong commitment to the principle that democratic participation is not merely a right but a civic duty.

The experiences of these countries provide valuable lessons on the impact of mandatory voting on electoral participation rates. For instance, Australia's implementation of compulsory voting in the early twentieth century led to a significant and sustained increase in voter turnout, which has remained consistently high ever since. This demonstrates the potential of mandatory voting to achieve its primary objective of maximising participation, thereby lending the electoral process and its outcomes greater legitimacy.

However, the global perspective on mandatory voting also highlights challenges and criticisms similar to those faced within any single nation contemplating its adoption. For example, the question of individual freedom versus civic duty is a recurring theme, with some arguing that the right to abstain is as fundamental as the right to vote. This philosophical debate underscores the importance of balancing the enforcement of mandatory voting with respect for individual liberties, a balance that varies across different jurisdictions.

The effectiveness of enforcement mechanisms is another area where global experiences diverge. In some countries, the penalties for non-compliance are strictly applied, leading to high compliance rates. In others, enforcement is more lenient or sporadic, raising questions about the consistency and fairness of the system. This variance offers insights into the importance of clear, fair, and consistently applied rules and penalties in achieving the objectives of mandatory voting without alienating the electorate.

The global landscape of mandatory voting reveals the critical role of public education and engagement strategies in ensuring that increased participation translates into more informed and meaningful electoral outcomes. Countries that have successfully combined compulsory voting with robust voter education campaigns tend to report not only higher turnout but also a more engaged and informed electorate. This underscores the importance of viewing mandatory voting not in isolation but as part of a broader strategy to enhance democratic engagement and literacy.

IMPLEMENT ONLINE VOTING SYSTEMS

The implementation of secure online voting systems in Australia presents an opportunity to modernise the electoral process, making it more accessible, convenient, and potentially increasing voter turnout. While the concept aligns with Australia's history of electoral innovation, it also brings challenges, particularly in terms of ensuring security and building public trust in the system. Drawing on both international examples and pilot programs within Australia can provide valuable insights and guidance. Successfully addressing these challenges is crucial for the effective implementation of online voting, with the goal of creating a more inclusive and representative democratic process.

THE HISTORICAL CONTEXT OF ELECTORAL INNOVATION IN AUSTRALIA

Australia's electoral system has long been recognised for its innovative approaches to democracy, setting a global precedent for practices designed to enhance fairness, inclusivity, and representation. The historical context of these innovations reveals a trajectory of progressive reforms that have significantly shaped the nation's democratic processes. However, in the latter half of the past century, there has been a perception that the pace of electoral innovation in Australia has decelerated, prompting discussions on the need for modernisation to align with contemporary technological advancements and societal expectations.

The introduction of compulsory voting marked a critical moment in Australia's electoral history. This move was aimed at addressing low voter turnout and ensuring that electoral outcomes reflected the will of a more comprehensive segment of society. The mandatory participation mandate underscored the nation's commitment to the principle that democracy is most robust and representative when all voices are heard. Similarly, the adoption of preferential voting systems further distinguished Australia's approach to elections. Unlike simple majority or first-past-the-post voting systems used in many other democracies, preferential voting allows voters to rank candidates by order of preference, ensuring that elected representatives have broader support beyond a mere plurality. These innovations underscored Australia's dedication to creating a more inclusive and representative electoral process, ensuring that the mechanisms of democracy evolved to better serve its citizens.

Despite these significant strides in electoral reform, there is a growing sentiment that Australia's pace of innovation in electoral processes has plateaued over the past 50 years. This period has seen fewer groundbreaking reforms, leading to discussions about how the Australian electoral system might further evolve to address contemporary challenges. Among these challenges are concerns about accessibility, engagement, and the integrity of the voting process in an increasingly digital and interconnected world.

The advent of the digital age presents both opportunities and challenges for electoral innovation. Online voting emerges as a potential next step in Australia's evolutionary path of electoral reform, aimed at leveraging technology to enhance accessibility and convenience for voters. Proponents argue that online voting could address some of the barriers to participation, such as physical disability, geographical remoteness, or time constraints, potentially increasing voter turnout and engagement. In an era where digital transactions have become commonplace, there is an argument to be made for modernising the voting process to reflect these technological advancements, making democracy more accessible and in tune with contemporary lifestyles.

However, the discussion around online voting and other potential electoral innovations also brings to light concerns about security, privacy, and the integrity of the electoral process. Ensuring the security of online voting systems against cyber threats, protecting voter privacy, and maintaining public trust in the fairness and accuracy of elections are paramount considerations. These challenges necessitate a careful and considered approach to innovation, balancing the potential benefits of modernisation with the imperative to uphold the integrity of the democratic process.

THE OBJECTIVES OF ONLINE VOTING IN AUSTRALIA

The objectives of implementing online voting in Australia encapsulate a forward-thinking approach to reimagining the electoral process in the digital age. With the aim of addressing contemporary challenges and barriers to voting, the move towards online voting is guided by principles of accessibility, convenience, and the potential to increase overall voter turnout. These objectives are not merely operational improvements but reflect a deeper commitment to enhancing democratic participation and ensuring that election outcomes are truly representative of the will of the people.

Enhanced accessibility stands at the forefront of the online voting initiative. Traditional voting methods, while effective to a degree, present obstacles for various segments of the population. Individuals with physical disabilities, for example, may find it difficult to navigate polling stations, even when these are designed to be accessible. Similarly, those living in remote or rural areas face logistical challenges in reaching polling stations, which can be located significant distances from their homes. Online voting proposes a solution to these challenges by enabling voters to cast their ballots from any location with internet access. This leap towards digital accessibility aims to dismantle the physical barriers that have historically disenfranchised certain groups, offering a more inclusive voting mechanism that aligns with principles of equal opportunity and participation.

Increased convenience is another pivotal objective underpinning the push for online voting. In the hustle and bustle of modern life, finding the time to visit a polling station can be a hurdle for people juggling work, family, and other commitments. This is particularly true in urban areas, where commuting can be time-consuming, and in situations where individuals are traveling or living abroad. Online voting addresses these issues by providing a more flexible and convenient voting option, allowing individuals to participate in the democratic process at a time and place that suits their schedules. By reducing the time and effort required to vote, online voting could significantly lower the barriers to participation, making the act of voting more compatible with contemporary lifestyles.

The potential for higher voter turnout is a consequential aim of introducing online voting. Australia generally records a higher voter turnout than many other countries, thanks to its mandatory voting legislation enacted in 1924. However, voter turnout at the 2022 federal election dipped to its lowest point since that time, with only 89 percent of eligible voters participating. This marked a significant decrease from the 96 percent turnout recorded at the 1996 federal election. By enhancing accessibility and convenience, online voting has the capacity to engage a broader cross-section of the electorate, including those who have been less likely to vote under traditional systems. Younger voters, who are accustomed to conducting various aspects of their lives online, might be particularly motivated by the ease and immediacy of online voting. Similarly, those who have felt disenfranchised or disconnected from the electoral process might find online voting a more approachable and engaging means of participation. Ultimately, the expectation is that by removing logistical hurdles and making voting more accessible, online voting could lead to higher participation rates, thereby ensuring that election outcomes more accurately reflect the preferences of a larger and more diverse portion of the electorate.

The objectives of implementing online voting in Australia revolve around a central theme of democratising access to the electoral process. By leveraging technology to enhance accessibility and convenience, online voting seeks to address the evolving needs and challenges of a modern, diverse society. The ultimate goal is to foster a more inclusive, participatory democracy where every eligible voter has the opportunity to have their voice heard, irrespective of physical, geographical, or temporal constraints. This vision for online voting represents a significant step towards modernising the Australian electoral system, reflecting a commitment to upholding the democratic principles of equal participation and representation in the digital age.

THE CHALLENGES IN IMPLEMENTING ONLINE VOTING IN AUSTRALIA

Implementing online voting in Australia represents a significant leap towards modernising the electoral process, promising greater accessibility and convenience for voters. However, the transition to digital voting is fraught with challenges that must be meticulously addressed to ensure the integrity, reliability, and acceptance of the system. These challenges encompass security concerns, the development of technological infrastructure, and the imperative of building and maintaining voter trust.

Security concerns emerge as the most pressing challenge in the realm of online voting. The digital nature of the process opens up new vulnerabilities, including the risk of hacking, fraud, and cyber-attacks. These threats are not merely hypothetical; they are real concerns that have been evidenced in various contexts around the globe, highlighting the need for an online voting system that is impervious to such risks. Ensuring the security and integrity of online voting systems requires a multifaceted approach, incorporating advanced encryption technologies, secure authentication methods, and continuous monitoring for potential threats. The challenge extends beyond preventing unauthorised access; it also involves safeguarding the system against internal vulnerabilities that could be exploited to alter votes or compromise the confidentiality of voter choices. Addressing these security concerns demands not only technological solutions but also a comprehensive legal and regulatory framework that establishes clear standards for online voting systems.

Technological infrastructure is another critical challenge in the implementation of online voting. Developing a platform that is both reliable and user-friendly necessitates significant investment in technology and infrastructure. This includes the servers and networks that will host the online voting system, as well as the software that enables the voting process. The infrastructure must be capable of handling high volumes of traffic without compromising performance, ensuring that all voters can access the system smoothly and without delays. The platform must be designed with all users in mind, incorporating accessibility features that accommodate voters with disabilities. The challenge extends to ensuring the system's resilience against potential failures, requiring robust backup and recovery procedures to protect against data loss or corruption. Addressing these technological requirements involves not only substantial financial resources but also expertise in cybersecurity, software development, and systems engineering.

Voter trust is indispensable to the successful implementation of online voting. Building and sustaining public confidence in the security and fairness of the online voting system is crucial. Voters need to be assured that their votes will be counted accurately and that their privacy will be protected. This challenge is compounded by the intangible nature of digital voting, where the physical act of casting a ballot is replaced by a virtual process. Addressing voter concerns about privacy and the potential for manipulation requires transparent communication about the measures in place to secure the system and protect voter information. It also involves educating the public about how online voting works, dispelling myths, and addressing misconceptions. Building voter trust is a continuous process that extends beyond the technical implementation of the system; it requires ongoing engagement with the electorate, responsiveness to concerns, and a commitment to transparency.

Cost is also an important factor in considering online voting. According to the Inquiry into and Report on All Aspects of the Conduct of the 2013 Federal Election and Matters Related Thereto, which was initiated following the loss of Senate ballot papers in Western Australia and explored online voting as remedy to the loss of ballot papers, the NSW iVote system used in the 2011 state election incurred an average cost of $74 per vote cast. This is in contrast to an average cost of $8 for all votes cast. However, as the system scales up to accommodate 200,000 voters, the cost per vote significantly decreases to an estimated average of $24. Clearly, as more electors access and use the system, this cost is expected to reduce further. Nonetheless, there are cost implications to consider when implementing a hybrid system that combines online methods with traditional pencil-and-paper approaches.

The success of online voting hinges on the ability to develop a system that not only meets the technical requirements of security and reliability but also earns the trust and confidence of voters and also taking into account that not everyone has the same access to technology, or the abilities to use technology for this purpose. The potential benefits of online voting—enhanced accessibility, convenience, and participation—remain a compelling vision for the future of democratic engagement in the digital age.

INTERNATIONAL EXAMPLES OF ONLINE VOTING

The exploration of online voting on the international stage offers a wide range of experiences, successes, and challenges that provide critical insights for countries such as Australia, considering embarking on similar digital electoral ventures. Countries and regions around the world have piloted or implemented online voting systems, each with its unique context, objectives, and outcomes. These international examples underscore the complexity of translating the concept of online voting into a functional, secure, and trusted component of the democratic process.

Estonia stands out as a pioneering example of online voting, having introduced the system for its parliamentary elections in 2005. As the first country to adopt online voting nationwide, Estonia's experience is particularly instructive. The key to its success lies in a comprehensive digital identity infrastructure, which allows secure and verifiable online transactions, including voting. Estonian citizens use a national ID card equipped with digital authentication and signing capabilities, facilitating a secure method to cast votes online. The Estonian model highlights the importance of a robust digital identity framework in underpinning secure and transparent online voting systems. Despite its success, Estonia's approach underscores the need for continuous vigilance and investment in cybersecurity measures to protect against evolving threats.

Switzerland has also experimented with online voting, with a focus on ensuring the system's transparency and security. Swiss online voting trials have emphasised the importance of verifiability, allowing voters to confirm that their vote has been recorded accurately while maintaining ballot secrecy. However, Switzerland's journey with online voting has faced hurdles, including the suspension of trials in some cantons due to security concerns. This experience illustrates the critical balance between advancing electoral convenience and ensuring the integrity of the voting process, highlighting the need for ongoing security assessments and the adaptability of the voting system to address identified vulnerabilities.

Norway embarked on online voting trials to increase electoral participation and explore the potential benefits of digital democracy. Conducted in select municipalities during national elections, Norway's foray into online voting was motivated by a desire to make voting more accessible, especially for citizens living abroad and those with disabilities. While the trials were deemed technically successful, concerns about security and the potential for coercion led to a cautious approach, with Norway not pursuing permanent online voting. Norway's experience reflects the importance of balancing technological innovation with concerns about voter privacy and the sanctity of the secret ballot.

From these international examples, several lessons emerge that are pertinent to Australia's contemplation of online voting. Security is paramount, with the need for continuous investment in cybersecurity measures to protect against external threats and ensure the integrity of the voting process. Transparency is essential in building and maintaining public trust in the online voting system. This involves clear communication about how the system works, how voter privacy is protected, and how votes are counted and verified. Voter education is also critical, as a well-informed electorate is better equipped to engage with online voting systems confidently and effectively. Education campaigns should address the mechanics of online voting, security features, and how voters can verify that their vote has been accurately recorded.

PILOT PROGRAMS AND TRIALS IN ONLINE VOTING

The introduction of online voting into the electoral landscape represents a significant shift in how democracies can facilitate the act of voting. Given the complexities and potential risks associated with transitioning to digital voting systems, the implementation of pilot programs and trials emerges as a prudent strategy. These preliminary steps serve not just as a testbed for technology but as an essential phase in building a robust, secure, and trustworthy online voting system. Conducting pilot programs and trials in local or state elections before nationwide implementation allows for a nuanced approach to identifying and resolving potential issues, building public trust, and refining the technology to meet the demands of a full-scale electoral process.

Pilot programs and trials offer the opportunity to evaluate the technical performance of online voting systems in a controlled environment. This includes assessing the system's ability to handle the volume of votes, its resistance to cyber threats, and the accuracy and integrity of the voting and counting processes. By starting small, any technical glitches or vulnerabilities can be addressed in a relatively low-stakes setting, preventing the kinds of problems that could undermine confidence in national elections. These trials also facilitate the gathering of data on user experience, highlighting areas where the voting interface may need improvements for accessibility, ease of use, and clarity. This iterative process of testing, feedback, and refinement is crucial in developing an online voting system that is not only secure but also user-friendly and inclusive.

Beyond technical considerations, pilot programs play a critical role in building public trust in online voting. Skepticism and concerns about the security and fairness of digital voting are natural, especially given the novelty of the process for many voters and the high stakes involved in electoral outcomes. By implementing trials in local or state elections, authorities can demonstrate in a transparent manner the measures taken to safeguard the voting process. This includes the encryption of votes, the anonymity of voters, and the verifiability of the results. Publicising the successes and lessons learned from these trials, as well as openly addressing any issues that arise, is key to fostering confidence among the electorate. Trust in online voting is built on a foundation of transparency, security, and reliability, qualities that pilot programs can help to establish and reinforce.

Pilot programs and trials provide invaluable insights into the broader implications of online voting on electoral participation. These initiatives can offer evidence on whether online voting leads to higher voter turnout, particularly among demographics that have traditionally faced barriers to voting. They also allow for the examination of the system's impact on the electoral process itself, including whether it influences the way voters engage with election campaigns and make their voting decisions. The findings from these trials can inform future decisions about the expansion of online voting, ensuring that such decisions are grounded in empirical evidence and a thorough understanding of the system's implications.

*

CHAPTER 2: CAMPAIGN FINANCE REFORM

PROVIDE FULL PUBLIC FUNDING OF ELECTIONS

Resistance to campaign finance reform in Australia, especially from the conservative side of politics, stems from a combination of perceived threats to established political advantages, concerns over free speech, the complexities of reform implementation, distrust in alternative funding mechanisms, and a general inertia within the political system. Despite the potential benefits of reform in enhancing public trust and improving political debate, these factors contribute to a slow and cautious approach to change. Skepticism about the effectiveness of reforms, fear of unintended consequences, and a lack of strong public demand for change further complicate efforts to overhaul campaign finance practices. This multifaceted resistance underscores the challenges of achieving significant reform in the political and regulatory landscape of campaign financing.

The debate over campaign finance reform in Australia presents a multifaceted narrative marked by resistance, apprehension, and complex socio-political undercurrents. At the heart of this resistance, especially pronounced on the conservative side of the political spectrum—the Liberal and National parties—lie several core concerns and perceptions that fuel this resistance, despite the acknowledged needs for enhanced transparency and equity in political financing.

The perceived threats to political advantage for the major political parties—albeit from the different perspectives of business support and union support—constitute a primary barrier to the embrace of campaign finance reform. Political parties and individuals who have navigated the currents of the existing system to their benefit harbour fears of losing their financial advantages over their main political rivals, and the entrant of smaller political parties. The prospect of reform introduces uncertainty, potentially dismantling the ability to significantly outspend opponents and thereby leveling the playing field in a manner that seems disadvantageous to those currently in positions of relative power and influence.

Entwined with practical concerns are ideological debates framing financial contributions as a facet of free speech and freedom of association. This argument posits that monetary support for political campaigns and causes represents a form of expression, an exercise of individual and organisational rights that should not be curtailed by stringent financial regulations. Such a perspective naturally leads to a resistance against reforms perceived to infringe upon these foundational democratic rights, setting the stage for a contentious battle over the limits of free expression in the realm of political finance.

The path to implementing comprehensive campaign finance reform is fraught with practical challenges that further fuel resistance and the complexity of crafting legislation that is both effective and enforceable, without introducing new loopholes or unintended consequences, is a daunting task. Skepticism regarding the efficacy of potential reform measures is widespread, rooted in concerns over the difficulty of enforcement and the risk that new regulations might inadvertently exacerbate existing issues or create entirely new problems within the political funding ecosystem.

Additionally, there exists a palpable distrust within the electorate about alternative funding mechanisms, such as increased public funding for political campaigns. Critics of such alternatives raise alarms over the potential for misuse of taxpayer funds and the introduction of new avenues for undue influence, undermining the intended goals of reform and perpetuating skepticism towards change.

Political systems, by their nature, tend toward inertia, exhibiting a preference for existing practices and norms. This bias is particularly pronounced in the domain of campaign finance, where entrenched interests and established financial networks resist disruption. The inertia is not only a byproduct of satisfaction with current conditions but reflects a deeper apprehension about the unknown ramifications of significant change.

Fear of unintended consequences further compounds resistance to campaign finance reform. The potential emergence of unregulated "dark money" and the shifting of funds into less transparent channels represent significant concerns that reform, however well-intentioned, might lead to outcomes more detrimental to the democratic process than those it seeks to ameliorate.

The lack of sustained and organised public pressure for reform plays a critical role in the slow pace of change. While surveys and polls may indicate public support for reform efforts, the absence of a cohesive, vocal demand for change limits the political motivation for lawmakers to pursue such reforms aggressively. Because of this, the interplay between public opinion and political action remains a critical, yet underleveraged, force in the campaign finance reform debate.

The resistance to campaign finance reform in Australia is underpinned by a complex collection of concerns, ranging from the protection of political advantages and free speech rights to the practical challenges of implementing change, distrust in alternatives, systemic inertia, fear of unintended consequences, and the lack of compelling public pressure. This confluence of factors creates a formidable barrier to reform, reflecting the intricate balance between maintaining the integrity of the democratic process and navigating the realities of political power dynamics.

THE OBJECTIVES OF PUBLIC FUNDING

Public funding of elections in Australia embodies a strategic approach aimed at bolstering democratic processes by mitigating the dependence of political candidates and parties on substantial private donations. At the heart of this initiative is the belief that a reduction in reliance on private funding sources is pivotal for curtailing potential undue influence from wealthy donors or organisations on political decisions and policies. This framework seeks to ensure that the political arena remains competitive and fair, allowing for a broader representation of the populace and fostering a healthier democratic environment.

The inception of public funding for elections in Australia traces back to the 1984, when the Hawke Labor government introduced public funding for political parties, with the intention that it would reduce the parties' reliance on corporate donations, in response to growing concerns over the transparency and integrity of political financing. The evolution of these funding mechanisms has been driven by the need to address disparities in financial resources among political entities, aiming to create a more level playing field. By providing financial support to eligible parties and candidates, the system aims to diminish the disparities that may exist due to varying abilities to attract private donations. This financial support is typically allocated based on previous electoral performance, ensuring that parties and candidates that have demonstrated a degree of public support are afforded the means to compete effectively.

The objectives of public funding are multi-faceted: besides reducing the influence of private funding, public funding aims

FIXING AUSTRALIAN POLITICS: HOW TO CHANGE THE SYSTEM OF GOVERNMENT

to enhance the accountability and transparency of political financing. By imposing strict reporting requirements and limits on expenditure, the system seeks to make the flow of money in politics more transparent, allowing voters to be better informed about the sources of political funding. This transparency is crucial for maintaining public trust in the electoral process, ensuring that voters can make informed decisions free from the shadow of financial influence.

In addition, public funding is designed to encourage participation from independents and smaller parties in the political process. By alleviating the financial burden on candidates and parties, the system enables a more diverse range of individuals to contemplate entering the political arena, including those who might otherwise be deterred by the high costs associated with campaigning. This diversification of political participation contributes to a more representative democracy, where a wider array of voices and perspectives can be heard and considered.

The absence of public funding for elections could lead to a significantly different political landscape in Australia. Without this mechanism, there would be an increased reliance on private donations, exacerbating the risks associated with undue influence and corruption. While wealthy individuals and organisations already wield significant political clout, especially in the field of minerals, mining and media interests, they could wield even more disproportionate power in the political sphere, skewing more policy and decision-making in their favour, leading to a further decline in public trust in the political process, as perceptions of fairness and impartiality are eroded.

IMPROVEMENT IN POLITICAL BEHAVIOUR

The extension of public funding—to full funding—into Australia's political landscape carries the promise of reshaping the dynamics of electoral competition and the very fabric of political engagement within the nation. By addressing the financial disparities that have historically skewed the electoral playing field, full public funding stands as a beacon of hope for a more equitable and representative political process. This financial mechanism not only levels the playing field but also enriches the democratic experience by fostering a political environment where ideas and policies, rather than financial muscle, determine the outcome of elections.

One of the virtues of full public funding is its potential to democratise political competition, and offers a lifeline to these underrepresented voices, providing them with the necessary resources to mount credible campaigns. This not only enhances the competitiveness of elections but also ensures that a wider spectrum of ideas and policies is presented to the electorate, enriching the democratic dialogue.

Full public funding can also act as a catalyst for improving the quality of political behaviour. In the absence of the relentless pursuit of private funds, candidates and parties can redirect their focus towards engaging with the electorate, understanding their concerns, and developing policies that address the needs of the broader community. This shift away from a fundraising-centric approach encourages a more issues-based campaign strategy, where the merits of policy proposals and the vision for the future become the primary focus. Such a transformation has the potential to foster a more informed and substantive political discourse, moving away from the sensationalism and superficiality that often plagues political campaigns in Australia. When was the last time a federal election—or any other election—felt like it was a salient opportunity to discuss the ideas that need to be introduced to address the many concerns of the electorate?

Public funding also holds the potential to mitigate the risks associated with undue influence and corruption. When political entities are less dependent on private donations, the opportunity for wealthy donors to exert undue influence over political decisions diminishes. This reduction in the potential for corruption not only enhances the integrity of the political process but also rebuilds public trust in political institutions. A political system that is perceived as fair and transparent is more likely to engender the confidence of the electorate, which is foundational to the health and sustainability of democracy.

The impact of public funding extends beyond the immediate electoral cycle. By enabling a broader range of candidates to participate in the political process, public funding contributes to a more diverse and representative political landscape and it is this diversity that is crucial for ensuring that the myriad voices and interests within society are adequately represented. When political representation mirrors the demographic and ideological diversity of the electorate, the policies and decisions emanating from political institutions are more likely to reflect the collective interests and values of the society they serve.

Public funding of elections in Australia represents a transformative approach to political engagement and governance. By extending the current system of campaign end election finances to a fully-fledged public funding model—at the exclusion of private funding—Australia can continue to evolve and strengthen its democracy, ensuring that it remains vibrant and responsive to the needs and aspirations of its citizens.

REDUCTION IN CORRUPTION RISKS IN AUSTRALIAN POLITICS

The extension of public funding into the electoral system of Australia emerges as a potent remedy against the malaise of corruption that can infiltrate the political arena, or remove corruption in the areas where it has already arrived. By creating a paradigm where reliance on private donations is significantly curtailed or removed entirely, the framework of public funding directly targets the vulnerabilities within the political system that predispose it to corrupt practices and the ensuing erosion of public trust. This strategic intervention seeks not only to diminish actual instances of corruption but also to address the public's perception of corruption, which is equally critical in maintaining the integrity and credibility of political institutions and the electoral process.

Corruption in politics, often stemming from the undue influence exerted by large private donations, undermines the democratic principles of fairness and equality. The potential for corruption arises when political decisions and policies become unduly influenced by the interests of a few wealthy donors or entities, rather than reflecting the collective will and welfare of the populace. In this context, public funding serves as a bulwark against such distortions of the democratic process. By providing a reliable and equitable source of funding to eligible political actors, public funding reduces their dependence on external, private sources of capital. This reduction in dependence not only lessens the opportunities for corrupt practices to take root but also attenuates the leverage that donors might seek to exert over political decision-making.

The proactive stance against corruption facilitated by public funding is reinforced by the robust regulatory frameworks that typically accompany such systems. These frameworks enforce strict rules regarding the disclosure of financial contributions and expenditures, ensuring a high degree of transparency. This transparency is instrumental in preventing corruption, as it subjects political financing to public scrutiny, making it more difficult for corrupt practices to go unnoticed. In addition, appropriate penalties associated with violating these regulations would serve as a significant deterrent against corruption, reinforcing the ethos of integrity within the political sphere.

The impact of reducing corruption through public funding extends beyond the immediate purview of financial transactions within the political system. At a more profound level, this approach plays a crucial role in restoring and enhancing public trust in political institutions and the electoral process. Trust in these institutions is the cornerstone upon which the legitimacy of democratic governance rests. When citizens believe that their political system is free from corruption and that political actors are acting in the public interest, their faith in the democratic process is strengthened. This trust is essential for the active and meaningful participation of citizens in democracy, encouraging them to engage with the political process, vote, and potentially seek political office themselves.

FINANCIAL THRESHOLDS FOR ELIGIBILITY

Thresholds for access to public funding for elections are designed with the dual aim of facilitating a fair and equitable distribution of funds to legitimate political actors, while simultaneously safeguarding against the potential exploitation of the system by non-viable candidates or parties.

Currently, the system mandates that political parties and candidates must attain a certain percentage of the total primary vote to qualify for public funding—4 per cent—and after this threshold has been reached, receive a specific amount per vote—in 2024, this amount for federal politics was $3.29 per eligible vote, and is indexed every six months. This requirement is predicated on the rationale that only those political entities that demonstrate a minimum level of public support should benefit from public resources. This threshold serves as a filter, ensuring that the allocation of public funds is directed towards those candidates and parties with a viable base of electoral support, thereby contributing to a more efficient and targeted use of public resources.

The debate around whether these financial thresholds should be amended—either increased or decreased—is multifaceted, touching upon principles of democratic fairness, the encouragement of political diversity, and the practical considerations of public finance management. On one hand, the argument for maintaining or even raising the current thresholds rests on the premise of fiscal responsibility.

By limiting eligibility for public funding to only those parties and candidates with substantial support, the system ensures that public funds are not dispersed too thinly across an excessively broad array of political entities, many of which may have minimal impact on the political landscape.

On the other hand, there is a compelling argument for lowering the financial thresholds, aimed at fostering a more inclusive and representative political environment. This perspective contends that by reducing the vote percentage required for eligibility, the system could better support emerging parties and independent candidates, encouraging a more vibrant and diverse political discourse. Such an adjustment could potentially lead to a more dynamic political arena, where new ideas and perspectives are given a platform, enhancing the democratic process by reflecting a wider array of societal views and interests.

The consideration of financial thresholds in public funding also raises questions about the role of public financing in leveling the playing field in politics. Lower thresholds could serve as an important mechanism for enabling smaller or newer political entities to compete more effectively against established parties with significant private fundraising capabilities. This could lead to a healthier democratic ecosystem, where the success of political entities is more closely tied to the strength of their ideas and policies, rather than their financial clout.

Any proposed amendments to the financial thresholds for public funding eligibility must be carefully considered, weighing the benefits of inclusivity and political diversity against the imperatives of fiscal prudence and the risk of diluting the impact of public funding. It is essential that such considerations are guided by a commitment to enhancing the democratic process, ensuring that any changes to the thresholds contribute to a more engaged, informed, and representative political landscape.

ENCOURAGE MICRO DONATIONS AND LIMIT THE BIG PLAYERS

Donation caps in Australian politics are a critical measure aimed at curtailing undue influence from wealthy individuals and organisations in political campaigns. By setting strict limits on the amount that can be donated, the system seeks to ensure a more equitable political arena where decisions and policies are guided by the interests of the broader public, not just the financially powerful.

These caps are complemented by comprehensive transparency and reporting requirements, which help maintain public trust in the electoral process. Effective enforcement and public education are also key components, ensuring that the caps are respected and understood. Implementing donation caps involves a delicate balance, requiring regular review and adjustment to remain effective against evolving campaign finance tactics and to continue promoting a healthy, democratic political environment.

REDUCE DONATION CAPS IN AUSTRALIAN POLITICS

The implementation of donation caps in Australian politics centres on a fundamental democratic principle: ensuring that the political system remains equitable and responsive to the entirety of its citizenry, rather than being unduly influenced by a select group of affluent donors. The rationale for instituting donation caps stems from a concern over the potential for significant financial contributions to skew the political process, allowing the wealthy to exercise a disproportionate level of influence over political decision-making and policy development. This concern is not merely theoretical; across various democracies, there has been evidence to suggest that without proper regulation, financial contributions can lead to a political landscape that prioritises the interests of the few over the many. Taking this into account, the introduction of donation caps is posited as a measure to prevent such imbalances, aiming to create a more level playing field in the political arena.

One of the primary advantages of implementing donation caps lies in its potential to democratise political influence. By limiting the amount that any individual or entity can donate to political parties or candidates, donation caps work to prevent the accumulation of undue influence by wealthy donors. This democratisation of influence ensures that political parties and candidates remain accountable to a broader base of the electorate, fostering a political environment where policies and decisions are more likely to reflect the collective interests of the populace rather than the narrow interests of the elite. Donation caps can also contribute to the reduction of corruption risks, as they limit the opportunities for financial contributions to be used as leverage for securing favourable policies or decisions from political figures.

Donation caps could also encourage a greater level of political engagement among the general populace. Knowing that the political playing field has been made more equitable through financial regulations may motivate more individuals to participate in the political process, whether through donations within the capped limits, voting, or even running for office. This heightened engagement is essential for the vitality of a democratic society, ensuring that its political system remains vibrant, representative, and responsive.

However, the implementation of donation caps also presents certain challenges and potential drawbacks. One concern is the risk of driving political donations into less transparent channels. If donors and political entities seek ways around the caps, this could lead to an increase in unreported or under-the-table financial contributions, undermining the very goal of enhancing transparency and accountability in political financing. There is also the argument that donation caps could inadvertently hamper the ability of political parties and candidates to fund robust campaigns. particularly for lesser-known candidates or emerging parties, where significant financial contributions can be crucial for building visibility and competing effectively against more established entities. In this view, donation caps could be seen as limiting political competition and diversity.

The question of how to best implement donation caps also involves a careful consideration of the specific limits to be set. Too low a cap might unduly restrict legitimate support for political entities, while too high a cap might fail to address the concerns of undue influence effectively. Therefore, the process of determining the appropriate levels for donation caps requires a nuanced understanding of the political landscape, as well as an ongoing dialogue among stakeholders to ensure that the caps achieve their intended objectives without unintended negative consequences.

TYPES OF POLITICAL DONATIONS COVERED IN AUSTRALIA

Donation caps in Australia traditionally apply to monetary contributions but advocating for a more inclusive approach that encompasses in-kind contributions, such as goods or services provided to political campaigns, is critical. This broadened scope is essential for a regulatory regime that fully encapsulates the various modes through which support and influence can be extended to political entities.

Including in-kind contributions under the umbrella of donation caps is instrumental in sealing potential loopholes that could be exploited to circumvent monetary caps. In-kind contributions, ranging from the provision of professional services without charge to the donation of goods or advertising space, can represent substantial support to a political campaign.

By valuing these contributions and applying caps accordingly, the regulatory framework ensures a more accurate and holistic control over the resources flowing into the political arena. This approach mitigates the risk of an uneven playing field, where significant support could be masked as in-kind contributions, thereby preserving the integrity of the caps.

The expansion of donation caps to include a wide array of contributions raises questions regarding its implications for freedom of association and political freedoms more broadly. Critics argue that imposing limits on the ways in which individuals and entities can support political causes may infringe upon fundamental democratic rights. From this perspective, the ability to contribute to political campaigns, whether through monetary donations or in-kind contributions, is seen as an essential expression of political engagement and support for democratic processes.

Addressing these concerns necessitates a careful balancing act— the goal of donation caps is not to stifle political participation or expression but to ensure that the political system is accessible and accountable to all, not just those with significant financial or material resources.

In this context, the design of donation caps should be sensitive to the importance of preserving individual freedoms while also safeguarding the democratic principle that political influence should not be disproportionately dictated by economic power.

To reconcile the objectives of preventing undue influence and preserving political freedoms, transparency and accountability become key. By ensuring that all types of contributions are transparently reported and subject to public scrutiny, the system can maintain oversight while respecting individuals' rights to support political causes. This transparency not only deters potential abuses but also fosters a more informed electorate, capable of discerning the influences shaping political campaigns and decisions.

Establishing clear guidelines for the valuation of in-kind contributions and ensuring that these guidelines are uniformly applied can help mitigate concerns about arbitrary limitations on political support. This clarity allows donors to understand the parameters within which they can contribute, ensuring that their support remains within the bounds of the law while still allowing for meaningful political engagement.

ENFORCEMENT AND PENALTIES FOR BREACHES IN DONATIONS

The integrity of the electoral process is a cornerstone of democratic governance, necessitating robust mechanisms to ensure adherence to funding and donation laws within Australian politics. Given the potential for breaches of these laws to undermine the fairness and transparency of elections, the establishment of suitable penalties for such violations is crucial. Effective enforcement mechanisms serve not only as a means to address infractions but also as a deterrent against the temptation to circumvent legal restrictions on electoral funding and donations. This dual role underscores the importance of designing a penalty framework that is both just and sufficiently stringent to discourage breaches.

Penalties for violating electoral funding and donation laws must be carefully calibrated to reflect the severity of the breach while ensuring that they serve as a real deterrent to both donors and recipients. Fines are a common and effective initial response, providing a financial disincentive against non-compliance. The scale of these fines should be significant enough to deter not just small-scale donors but also larger entities for whom a nominal fine might not present a substantial deterrent. This implies a sliding scale of fines that can be adjusted based on the severity of the breach, the amount by which donations exceed legal caps, and whether the breach is part of a repeated pattern of behaviour.

Beyond financial penalties, more severe legal repercussions are necessary for serious or repeated violations. These could include criminal charges leading to potential imprisonment for the most egregious breaches, such as deliberate attempts to evade donation caps through fraudulent means or the wilful failure to disclose significant contributions. The imposition of criminal penalties underscores the seriousness with which breaches of electoral funding and donation laws are viewed, emphasising the critical importance of these laws to the maintenance of a fair and transparent electoral system.

For political parties or candidates found in violation, additional sanctions could be applied to directly address their electoral ambitions. These might include the suspension of their eligibility for public funding, a ban on participating in the next electoral cycle, or the annulment of election results in cases where breaches have had a demonstrable impact on the outcome. Such penalties not only punish the offending parties but also serve to protect the integrity of the electoral process by ensuring that those who benefit from breaches of funding and donation laws do not enjoy the fruits of their misconduct.

The enforcement of these penalties requires a robust and independent oversight body with the authority and resources to investigate alleged breaches, impose penalties, and, where necessary, refer cases to either the National Commission Against Corruption for further investigation or, if required, the courts for criminal prosecution. This body must operate with a high degree of transparency and accountability to maintain public trust in its impartiality and effectiveness.

However, the implementation of penalties must also be guided by principles of fairness and due process. Accused parties should have the opportunity to respond to allegations, and penalties should be imposed only where there is clear evidence of wrongdoing. This approach ensures that the enforcement regime is not only tough but also just, reflecting a balanced application of the law that respects individual rights while vigorously protecting the public interest.

PUBLIC SUPPORT AND EDUCATION FOR ELECTORAL AND POLITICAL REFORM IN AUSTRALIA

In the quest for electoral and political reform in Australian politics, public support and education emerge as central forces. These elements are not merely adjunct to the legal and regulatory frameworks established to govern electoral conduct but are fundamental to the success and sustainability of such reforms. The cultivation of public awareness and understanding regarding the intricacies of electoral and political reform, such as the rationale behind donation caps, plays a critical role in securing a broad base of support for these measures. It is through this informed engagement that the public can transition from passive observers of the political process to active and vigilant participants, ensuring that the principles of democratic integrity are upheld.

The pathway to harnessing public support and education for electoral and political reform involves several strategic initiatives, especially in the development and deployment of comprehensive public awareness campaigns. These campaigns would be designed to elucidate the purpose and benefits of reforms, such as donation caps, explaining how they serve to protect the democratic process from undue influence and ensure a level playing field for all participants. By demystifying the objectives and mechanisms of these reforms, such campaigns can dispel misconceptions and foster a positive perception of the changes among the electorate.

Education plays a synergistic role with awareness campaigns, delving deeper into the substance of the reforms. Educational initiatives can be integrated into the curriculum at various levels of the education system, ensuring that citizens are equipped from an early age with a robust understanding of the democratic process and the importance of fairness and integrity within this system. Additionally, public forums, workshops, and online resources can offer opportunities for ongoing education, enabling the electorate to remain informed about developments in electoral and political reform.

Leveraging media platforms to disseminate information and foster dialogue about electoral and political reform is also essential. The media, in its various forms, has the power to reach a wide audience, providing a platform for debate, discussion, and the exchange of ideas. By engaging with the media, proponents of reform can ensure that the discourse surrounding these issues remains vibrant and accessible to the broader public.

The promotion of public support and education for electoral and political reform also involves addressing potential resistance or skepticism. By providing clear, evidence-based arguments and demonstrating the tangible benefits of reforms, it is possible to build a compelling case that resonates with the values and aspirations of the Australian populace. This approach underscores the principle that democratic reforms are not merely technical adjustments but are fundamental to the preservation and enhancement of the democratic ideals that underpin the nation.

MANAGE POLITICAL DONATIONS IN THE PUBLIC INTEREST

Enhancing transparency in the funding of political parties in Australia through the real-time public disclosure of donations and expenditures is critical for ensuring accountability and maintaining public trust in the political system. This approach involves the comprehensive and immediate reporting of financial activities related to political campaigns, utilising digital technologies to facilitate access to information. Independent oversight bodies play a pivotal role in monitoring compliance and enforcing rules, while public education initiatives help to engage the populace in the importance of transparency. By adopting these measures, Australia can work towards a more transparent, accountable, and trustworthy political funding system, drawing on international best practices to continuously improve and adapt its approach.

REAL-TIME DONATION DISCLOSURES

In the era of digital transformation, the potential for leveraging technology to enhance transparency and accountability in political financing has never been greater. Real-time disclosure of political donations represents a critical innovation in this field, promising to redefine the landscape of electoral integrity in Australia. By mandating that information about political donations and expenditures be made available to the public as they occur, this approach aims to fortify the democratic process against the risks of undue influence and corruption. The deployment of computer and online digital mechanisms for real-time disclosure can play a crucial role in achieving this goal, offering a blend of immediacy, accessibility, and transparency that traditional reporting methods cannot match.

The foundation of real-time disclosure systems in the digital domain is the development and implementation of a centralised online platform. This platform would serve as the repository for all data related to political donations and expenditures, accessible by the public at any time. To ensure the effectiveness of this system, it would need to be designed with user-friendly interfaces that allow for easy navigation and interpretation of the data. Features could include search functions that enable users to look up donations by donor, recipient, amount, and date, as well as visualisation tools that help illustrate trends and patterns in political financing.

Behind the scenes, the success of a real-time disclosure platform depends on the integration of robust data processing and management technologies. Automated systems for data entry and verification are essential to handle the volume of transactions and ensure their accuracy. These systems could include application programming interfaces that allow political parties and donors to directly upload their donation information into the platform, reducing the lag time between the occurrence of a donation and its public disclosure. To maintain the integrity of the data, sophisticated algorithms could be employed to detect and flag anomalies or discrepancies for further investigation.

Blockchain technology presents another innovative avenue for enhancing the reliability and security of real-time disclosure systems. By recording transactions on a decentralised ledger, blockchain offers a tamper-proof record of political donations and expenditures, ensuring that once a piece of data is entered, it cannot be altered retrospectively. This characteristic addresses concerns about the manipulation of donation records, providing an additional layer of confidence in the transparency of the political financing process.

The real-time disclosure of political donations also necessitates considerations of privacy and data protection. While the goal is to maximise transparency, it is important to balance this with the need to protect sensitive personal information. Implementing strict data security protocols and anonymising certain details without compromising the utility of the information can help achieve this balance.

The effectiveness of real-time disclosure systems extends beyond the technology itself to encompass the regulatory and legal framework within which they operate. Legislation mandating timely and comprehensive reporting of political donations and expenditures is critical to ensure compliance. Equally important is the role of oversight bodies in monitoring the system, enforcing regulations, and addressing any issues that arise. The success of real-time disclosure initiatives will depend on the thoughtful integration of technology, regulation, and public engagement, ensuring that the system is not only technologically robust but also supported by a legal framework and cultural commitment to transparency.

WHAT SHOULD BE THE SCOPE OF DISCLOSURE?

Within all of the complex factors within political finances, the thorough monitoring and reporting of political donations is paramount to safeguarding the integrity of democratic processes. The challenge lies not only in the tracking of traditional financial contributions but also in the comprehensive coverage of a broad spectrum of financial activities that could potentially sway political influence. This requires a multifaceted strategy that encompasses direct financial donations, in-kind contributions, campaign expenditures, and other forms of financial support. By adopting a holistic approach to disclosure, the potential avenues for undue influence can be meticulously monitored and reported, preserving the foundational principles of transparency and accountability in the political domain.

Central to the efficacy of this strategy is the establishment of a robust framework for monitoring that is both adaptive and inclusive. This framework must be equipped to capture the full array of financial activities associated with political campaigns, including emerging and non-traditional forms of fundraising and support. The diversity of these activities necessitates a dynamic monitoring system that can evolve in response to the changing landscape of political finance. For instance, digital platforms have emerged as significant mediums for fundraising, expanding the traditional boundaries of political donations to include online contributions, crowdfunding initiatives, and social media campaigns. Recognising and integrating these digital fundraising activities into the monitoring framework is crucial for ensuring comprehensive coverage.

The reporting mechanism plays a critical role in the transparency and accountability process, serving as the conduit through which monitored information is communicated to the public, regulatory bodies, and other stakeholders. Effective reporting entails not just the timely and accurate disclosure of financial activities but also the presentation of this information in an accessible and understandable format. Leveraging technology to facilitate real-time reporting can significantly enhance the immediacy and relevance of disclosed information. Online databases and platforms that offer user-friendly access to financial disclosures empower citizens, watchdog organisations, and the media to scrutinise political financing, fostering an environment of informed public oversight.

The inclusion of in-kind contributions in the disclosure requirements marks a significant expansion of the monitoring scope. Valuing these non-monetary donations, such as volunteered professional services, donated goods, or provided venues for campaign events, presents unique challenges. Developing standardised methodologies for the valuation and reporting of in-kind contributions is essential to ensure that their potential impact on political influence is transparently and accurately represented.

In addition to domestic efforts, there is value in considering international best practices and multinational co-operative initiatives that enhance the global standards of political finance transparency. Engaging in dialogue and sharing experiences with other democracies can provide valuable insights and innovative approaches to addressing common challenges in monitoring and reporting political donations.

INDEPENDENT OVERSIGHT OF DONATIONS AND ELECTORAL FUNDING

The Australian Electoral Commission currently plays a significant role in the administration of electoral processes, including aspects of political finance. However, the evolving landscape of political donations and funding, characterised by increasing complexity and sophistication, calls for a reassessment of the mechanisms and bodies in place for oversight.

The question arises whether the AEC, either in its current form or with augmented powers and resources, could suffice as the sole guardian of transparency and integrity in political finance, or whether the establishment of a new, specialised entity might better serve the Australian political system.

An effective oversight body, whether it be an enhanced AEC or a newly established entity—in co-ordination with the National Commission Against Corruption—must be endowed with a robust set of powers and capabilities to ensure the rigorous enforcement and monitoring of disclosure rules. This includes the authority to conduct comprehensive audits of political entities' financial records, investigate allegations of non-compliance, and impose penalties for violations. Such powers are crucial for deterring misconduct and ensuring adherence to the legal and regulatory framework governing political donations and electoral funding.

The independence of this oversight body is a non-negotiable issue—it must operate free from political influence to maintain the trust of the public and ensure that its actions are guided solely by the principles of fairness and integrity. This independence is not only a matter of structural and operational design but also of perception; the credibility of the oversight body in the eyes of the electorate is foundational to its effectiveness.

The scope of the oversight body's mandate must also be comprehensive, encompassing all forms of political donations and funding. This includes not only traditional monetary contributions but also in-kind donations, third-party campaigning, and other indirect forms of financial support.

By covering the full spectrum of political finance activities, the oversight body can provide a holistic safeguard against the risks of undue influence.

In terms of improvement, there should be an emphasis on enhancing the technological capabilities of the oversight body. In the digital age, the use of advanced data analytics, blockchain for secure and transparent record-keeping, and online platforms for real-time disclosure can significantly augment the effectiveness of monitoring and enforcement efforts. Such technological advancements can also facilitate greater public engagement with the oversight process, empowering citizens to play a more active role in holding political entities accountable.

The establishment or enhancement of an independent body for overseeing donations and electoral funding in Australian politics must be accompanied by a commitment to ongoing review and adaptation. As the methods and modalities of political finance evolve, so too must the mechanisms for oversight. This requires not only a foundational legal and regulatory framework but also a culture of vigilance, innovation, and public engagement.

The cumulative effect of enhanced transparency and accountability in political financing would also result in a gradual improvement in trust among the electorate, and trust in political institutions and processes is fundamental to the health and vitality of a democracy. When the electorate believes that political campaigns are conducted fairly, with financial transparency and accountability, it bolsters their confidence in the democratic system. This trust is not merely abstract; it translates into greater electoral participation, more constructive political engagement, and a deeper commitment to democratic ideals.

INTERNATIONAL BEST PRACTICES FOR DONATIONS, ELECTION FUNDING AND FUNDING REFORM

The global landscape of democratic governance presents a rich experience of approaches to managing donations, electoral funding, and the ongoing quest for funding reform. Each nation's unique historical, political, and social contexts have shaped distinct mechanisms and regulations designed to ensure the integrity of political financing. Australia, in its efforts to refine and enhance its system of transparency and accountability in political donations and electoral funding, stands to gain valuable insights from the examination of international best practices. While acknowledging that no system is flawless, the comparative analysis of global practices offers a reservoir of ideas for innovation and improvement.

One illustrative example is the model adopted by several Scandinavian countries, such as Sweden and Norway, which emphasises public funding for political parties alongside strict controls and caps on private donations. This approach seeks to level the playing field among political entities, reducing the risk of undue influence from wealthy donors. The transparency and regular public reporting inherent in these systems serve as a deterrent against corruption, ensuring that political financing remains in the public eye. Australia could consider the balance achieved in these nations between public financing and private contributions, exploring ways to enhance its public funding mechanisms to diminish the reliance on private donations.

Germany's mixed approach to political financing offers another compelling model. It combines state funding with private donations, but with a unique matching funds system, where the state matches the amount raised by parties through small individual contributions up to a certain limit. This incentivises parties to engage with a broader base of small donors, rather than relying on a few large donations. The German model, with its emphasis on transparency and stringent reporting requirements, underscores the potential benefits of encouraging wider public participation in political financing. Such a system could inspire reforms in Australia aimed at bolstering small-scale donations while maintaining rigorous transparency standards.

The United States presents a different scenario, characterised by high levels of private funding and sophisticated regulatory mechanisms for disclosure, managed by the Federal Election Commission. Despite criticisms concerning the influence of money in politics, the U.S. system offers valuable lessons on the technological and procedural aspects of real-time donation reporting and the management of third-party expenditures. The comprehensive online databases and the use of digital platforms for instant disclosure in the U.S. could inform Australian efforts to enhance the accessibility and timeliness of its own reporting systems.

Canada's approach to political donations and funding reform, particularly its restrictions on corporate and union donations alongside caps on individual contributions, represents a concerted effort to limit potential sources of undue influence. In addition, Canada's enforcement framework, including the roles and powers of the Election Commissioner, provides a robust model for investigating and penalising breaches of political finance laws. This aspect of the Canadian system could offer guidance to Australia in strengthening its enforcement mechanisms to ensure compliance with funding and donation regulations.

Drawing from these international examples, several key themes emerge that could guide Australia in its pursuit of more effective management of political donations and electoral funding. The importance of a balanced approach that incorporates both public funding and regulated private contributions, the incentivisation of small-scale donations, the adoption of advanced technological tools for real-time disclosure, and the establishment of strong enforcement mechanisms stand out as critical elements for reform.

In synthesising these international best practices, Australia must consider its unique political culture and democratic values. Adaptation and customisation of these practices will be necessary to align with Australian legal and societal norms. Any reforms adopted should be subject to continuous evaluation and refinement, with the flexibility to evolve in response to new challenges and developments in political financing. Through a thoughtful and informed approach to reform, inspired by global best practices, Australia can enhance the transparency, integrity, and accountability of its political financing system, reinforcing the foundations of its democracy.

*

CHAPTER 3: ENHANCING TRANSPARENCY AND ACCOUNTABILITY

TIGHTEN CORRUPTION MEASURES

Reforming Australian politics to combat corruption more effectively requires a comprehensive overhaul and strengthening of existing anti-corruption measures, especially in consideration of the National Anti-Corruption Commission, which was formed on 1 July 2023. By evaluating and enhancing the NACC's independence, investigative and prosecutorial powers, and ensuring greater protection for whistleblowers, Australia can create a more resilient and transparent political system. Public engagement and interagency cooperation are also crucial in fostering a culture of integrity and accountability. Periodic reviews will ensure these measures remain effective and adaptable to new challenges. Together, these steps will significantly enhance the ability to detect, investigate, and prosecute political corruption in Australia.

ASSESSMENT OF THE NATIONAL ANTI-CORRUPTION COMMISSION

The establishment of the National Anti-Corruption Commission marked a significant step towards addressing the persistent issue of corruption within the political system. However, assessing the effectiveness and limitations of such a body, especially given its recent inception, requires a nuanced understanding of its roles, powers, and the context within which it operates. While it can be argued that it is too early to evaluate the NACC's impact thoroughly, initial observations and analyses can offer insights into its potential trajectory and areas where enhancements may be necessary.

At its core, the NACC was conceived to provide a robust framework for investigating and mitigating corruption across various levels of government. The commission's establishment was a response to growing public demand for greater accountability and transparency in political and governmental affairs. To understand its effectiveness, it is imperative to examine its jurisdiction, which ideally should encompass a wide range of corrupt activities, from bribery and embezzlement to more subtle forms of influence peddling and nepotism. The breadth and depth of the NACC's jurisdiction are crucial determinants of its ability to address corruption comprehensively.

Equally important are the powers granted to the NACC. These powers determine not just the scope of its investigative capabilities but also its capacity to hold individuals and entities accountable. The ability to conduct investigations autonomously, compel testimony, and prosecute or refer cases for prosecution are fundamental to an anti-corruption agency's success. Without sufficient powers, even the most well-intentioned body may find itself hamstrung, unable to address the very issues it was created to combat.

Resources and autonomy are two additional critical factors in the assessment of the NACC. Adequate funding, access to expertise, and technological resources are essential for conducting thorough investigations and operating effectively. Furthermore, the commission's autonomy from political influences is a litmus test for its integrity and effectiveness. An anti-corruption agency must operate independently to maintain public trust and ensure that its actions are guided solely by the pursuit of justice, free from political considerations.

Early challenges are to be expected as the commission navigates its mandate, establishes procedures, and builds its reputation. However, this initial period is also critical for setting precedents, establishing public confidence, and demonstrating a commitment to tackling corruption without fear or favour.

Given its recent establishment, a definitive assessment of the NACC's effectiveness may indeed be premature, although at of 31 December 2023, it had received 2,327 referrals, of which 537 have deemed to be referrals worthy of further investigation.

ENHANCING INDEPENDENCE

The integrity and efficacy of anti-corruption bodies are fundamentally anchored in their ability to operate with unassailable independence from political influence. The cornerstone of public trust in these institutions lies in their perceived and actual autonomy, ensuring that their investigations and actions are guided solely by the principles of justice and accountability, rather than political expediency. Enhancing the independence of these bodies is not just a matter of structural adjustment but a profound commitment to the foundational values of democracy and the rule of law.

Securing independent funding is a critical step in fortifying the autonomy of anti-corruption bodies. By establishing a funding mechanism that is insulated from political manipulation, such as direct allocations from the legislature with statutory protections against arbitrary adjustments, these bodies can avoid the pitfalls of financial coercion. This ensures that their operational capabilities are not hampered by budgetary constraints imposed as a means of influencing their activities or diluting their investigations.

The process of appointing commissioners to anti-corruption bodies is another critical aspect that demands meticulous attention. Implementing a transparent and merit-based selection process is essential to avoid the appointment of individuals based on political loyalty or affiliations, which could compromise the institution's impartiality. This process should involve clear criteria for eligibility that prioritise integrity, expertise in law enforcement, legal practice, or public administration, and a demonstrable commitment to anti-corruption efforts. The involvement of a diverse panel in the selection process, including members from the judiciary, civil society, and possibly bipartisan parliamentary committees, can enhance the credibility and impartiality of the appointments.

Safeguarding commissioners and staff against unjust removal is equally vital. Protections against arbitrary dismissal are crucial for empowering anti-corruption officials to pursue their duties without fear of retribution. Such protections could include specifying tenures for commissioners and setting high thresholds for their removal, such as requiring a supermajority vote in the legislature or the substantiation of misconduct through judicial review. These measures ensure that the tenure of anti-corruption officials is shielded from the vicissitudes of political fortunes and partisan considerations.

The independence of anti-corruption bodies is a bulwark against the erosion of democratic institutions and the entrenchment of corruption. It signifies a commitment to the principles that underpin a fair and just society, where public officials are held to account, and the public trust is safeguarded. By implementing measures to secure funding, ensure transparent and merit-based appointments, and protect against unjust removal, Australia can fortify the independence of its anti-corruption bodies. This not only enhances their capacity to combat corruption effectively but also reaffirms the nation's dedication to upholding the highest standards of integrity and governance.

EXPANDING INVESTIGATIVE POWERS

The delicate balance of empowering anti-corruption bodies with expansive investigative powers, while ensuring these powers do not become excessively dominant, is a nuanced challenge. The goal is to enhance these bodies' effectiveness in unearthing and addressing corruption, which necessitates granting them significant capabilities, such as compelling evidence, conducting hearings, and initiating investigations autonomously. However, it is equally important to institute safeguards that prevent the overreach of these powers, and maintaining a balanced approach that upholds justice and protects civil liberties.

Expanding the investigative powers of anti-corruption bodies to compel evidence is a critical step in fortifying their ability to thoroughly investigate corruption allegations. This power would enable the anti-corruption bodies to obtain necessary documents, data, and testimonies that are vital for piecing together the complex jigsaw of corrupt practices. However, to ensure that this power is not misused, it must be accompanied by strict judicial oversight. For instance, the commission could be required to obtain a warrant or a similar judicial approval when its requests for information intrude upon individual privacy or business confidentiality, providing a check on its authority.

The capability to conduct both public and private hearings is another aspect that could significantly enhance the investigative process. Public hearings play a crucial role in maintaining transparency, educating the public on the workings of corruption, and restoring public trust in the system. Meanwhile, private hearings are essential for protecting sensitive information and the identities of those involved, whether as witnesses or whistleblowers. Implementing criteria that dictate when each type of hearing is appropriate can ensure that the decision to hold a hearing in public or private balances the public interest with the rights of those involved.

Granting anti-corruption bodies the autonomy to initiate investigations without needing a referral from government entities addresses a significant barrier to proactive anti-corruption efforts. This independence is crucial for investigating corruption without bias or delay. Nonetheless, to prevent potential abuse of this power, there should be clear guidelines defining the circumstances under which investigations can be initiated, including credible evidence thresholds and oversight mechanisms to review the decision to investigate.

Establishing an independent oversight committee to review the exercise of these expanded powers regularly could serve as an effective safeguard. This committee could be composed of members from diverse backgrounds, including the judiciary, legal experts, and representatives from civil society, ensuring a broad perspective on the anti-corruption body's actions.

PROSECUTORIAL AUTHORITY

In the ongoing efforts to enhance the efficacy of anti-corruption frameworks within Australia, a significant consideration is the potential expansion of prosecutorial authority for bodies such as the National Anti-Corruption Commission. This proposition entails either endowing these agencies with the power to directly prosecute corruption cases or, alternatively, refining the process through which cases are referred to prosecutorial services. Such a move aims to streamline the fight against corruption by eliminating procedural bottlenecks and ensuring a more direct path from investigation to prosecution. However, this proposition carries with it a spectrum of implications, both positive and negative, that warrant a thorough examination.

The potential benefits of granting prosecutorial authority to anti-corruption bodies are manifold. Primarily, it could significantly expedite the legal process by removing layers of bureaucracy involved in transferring cases from an investigative agency to the prosecutorial system. This direct line from investigation to prosecution would ideally reduce delays, ensuring swift justice and serving as a stronger deterrent against corrupt activities. Furthermore, anti-corruption agencies with prosecutorial powers could ensure a higher degree of specialisation and expertise in handling corruption cases, given their focused mandate and accumulated experience in this domain.

The expansion of prosecutorial powers, however, is not without its concerns. One of the most significant risks is the potential for such bodies to become overly powerful, creating an imbalance within the legal and democratic framework. With the ability to both investigate and prosecute, there could be fewer opportunities for external review and checks on the agency's decisions, raising fears of unjust prosecutions or the misuse of power. The concentration of investigative and prosecutorial powers in a single entity might also lead to perceptions of bias, undermining the public's trust in the fairness and impartiality of the justice process.

There are practical considerations related to the implementation of such a change. Providing prosecutorial authority to an existing agency like the NACC would require significant structural and procedural adjustments, including the provision of additional resources and legal expertise to fulfill this expanded role effectively. It would also necessitate a re-evaluation of the mechanisms for oversight and accountability to ensure that the agency's expanded powers are exercised responsibly.

An alternative to granting direct prosecutorial powers is the enhancement of the existing mechanism for referring cases to prosecutorial services. This approach seeks to streamline and strengthen the collaboration between investigative and prosecutorial bodies without concentrating too much power in the hands of the former. By establishing clear protocols, timelines, and communication channels, the process can be made more efficient, addressing concerns about delays and obstruction of justice while maintaining a separation of powers that safeguards democratic principles.

INTERAGENCY COOPERATION

Interagency cooperation represents a cornerstone in the multifaceted strategy to combat corruption effectively within Australia. The collaborative synergy between the NACC, law enforcement bodies, and other relevant agencies is essential for creating a comprehensive and cohesive approach to identifying, investigating, and prosecuting corrupt activities. However, while the benefits of such cooperation are evident, it raises pertinent questions about the balance of power within the government and the potential risks of excessive governmental authority in the fight against corruption.

The merits of enhanced interagency cooperation are extensive. By fostering a culture of collaboration and open communication, agencies can leverage a wealth of diverse expertise, resources, and intelligence capabilities. This unified approach enables a more holistic view of the corruption landscape, facilitating the identification of patterns and connections that might elude isolated entities.

Coordinated efforts can streamline investigations, prevent duplicative work, and ensure a more efficient use of public resources. Through shared strategies and joint operations, agencies can also tackle sophisticated corruption schemes that transcend the jurisdictional boundaries of any single organisation.

Notwithstanding these advantages, the intensification of interagency cooperation must be navigated with caution to avoid the concentration of too much power in the hands of the government. One potential concern is the risk of creating an overly intrusive state apparatus that could infringe on individual freedoms and privacy under the guise of combating corruption. There is a fine line between thorough investigation and overreach, and without clear boundaries, there's a risk that such powers could be misused against political opponents, whistleblowers, or civil society groups under the broad umbrella of anti-corruption efforts.

To mitigate these risks, it is imperative to establish robust oversight mechanisms and legal safeguards that govern the extent and nature of interagency cooperation. Transparency in the operations of anti-corruption efforts must be maintained to ensure public accountability. This could involve legislative oversight, judicial review, and mechanisms for public scrutiny and feedback on the activities of anti-corruption agencies. The principle of proportionality should guide the extent of cooperation and information sharing, ensuring that actions taken are necessary and directly related to the investigation of corruption, with adequate protections for individual rights and privacy.

Another critical aspect is the establishment of formal frameworks and agreements that delineate the parameters of interagency cooperation. These frameworks should specify the roles and responsibilities of each agency, the procedures for information sharing, and the mechanisms for resolving conflicts or jurisdictional disputes. By clearly defining the scope and limits of collaborative efforts, such agreements can help prevent overreach and ensure that cooperation enhances, rather than undermines, the democratic governance structure.

PERIODIC REVIEW AND ADAPTATION

In the dynamic landscape of governance and public administration, the fight against corruption demands not only vigilance but also an adaptive and proactive approach. The proposition to legislate regular reviews of anti-corruption legislation and bodies every decade reflects a deep understanding of the mutable nature of corruption itself. Such periodic evaluations are essential for ensuring that the legislative and institutional frameworks remain effective, relevant, and resilient against both current and emerging forms of corrupt practices.

Corruption, by its nature, evolves continuously, adapting to new regulations, exploiting loopholes, and finding safe havens within the existing legal and institutional frameworks. This chameleon-like characteristic of corruption necessitates a similarly dynamic response from anti-corruption strategies. Regular, legislated reviews offer a structured approach to assess the efficacy of anti-corruption measures, identify areas of weakness, and adapt to changing circumstances. This process ensures that legislation keeps pace with the innovative tactics of corruption, and anti-corruption bodies are equipped with the necessary tools and mandates to address these challenges effectively.

Legislating these reviews acknowledges the importance of institutionalising the process, ensuring it is not left to the discretion of transient political will or priorities. A legislated mandate provides a regular, systematic evaluation mechanism that transcends political cycles, offering continuity and stability to the anti-corruption efforts. It signals a commitment to a sustained fight against corruption that is not subject to the vicissitudes of political agendas.

A timeframe for reviews—once a decade—strikes a balance between the need for stability and the necessity for adaptation. It allows enough time for policies and initiatives to be implemented and their impacts to be observed and assessed, while also ensuring that the legal and institutional frameworks do not become outdated in the face of rapidly evolving corrupt practices. This timeframe also provides an opportunity for a comprehensive and thoughtful review process, involving extensive consultation with stakeholders, experts, and the public, fostering a participatory approach to reform.

However, the effectiveness of these periodic reviews hinges on several key factors. First, the review process must be genuinely independent, free from political interference, to ensure that its findings and recommendations are unbiased and focused solely on enhancing the anti-corruption framework. Second, there must be a clear and actionable mechanism for implementing the recommendations arising from the review. Without the political and institutional will to enact necessary reforms, the reviews risk becoming mere formalities without tangible impact.

While ten-year reviews provide a structured approach to evaluating and adapting anti-corruption measures, they must be complemented by more frequent assessments and monitoring. The rapidly changing nature of corruption and the political, economic, and technological environments in which it operates may require more agile responses than those afforded by a ten-year cycle. As a result, embedding flexibility within the review process to allow for interim evaluations in response to significant developments is crucial.

INTERNATIONAL ANTI-CORRUPTION AGENCIES AS A MODEL

Many countries employ a diverse array of anti-corruption strategies and frameworks, reflecting the unique political, social, and economic contexts in which they operate. Australia's approach to combating corruption, characterised by a combination of robust legislative frameworks, independent anti-corruption agencies, and a strong rule of law, places it among the countries actively engaged in this battle. However, when comparing Australia's anti-corruption measures with those of other nations, it becomes evident that the effectiveness of anti-corruption efforts is falling behind and could significantly benefit from innovative practices and strategies implemented worldwide.

Internationally, some countries stand out for their exemplary anti-corruption efforts, offering valuable lessons and best practices. For instance, the Scandinavian countries, notably Denmark, Finland, and Sweden, consistently rank high on Transparency International's Corruption Perceptions Index. These countries attribute their success to a strong culture of transparency, comprehensive public sector regulations, high levels of civic engagement, and efficient public services that are resistant to corruption. The key takeaway from the Scandinavian model is the importance of fostering a culture of integrity and transparency throughout society, coupled with effective public administration that minimally relies on bureaucratic discretion, which can often be a hotbed for corrupt practices.

Singapore offers another exemplary case, renowned for its stringent anti-corruption laws and the effectiveness of its Corrupt Practices Investigation Bureau. Singapore's approach is characterised by strong political will to combat corruption, comprehensive anti-corruption legislation, and severe penalties for corrupt activities, regardless of the individual's status or position. The CPIB operates with a high degree of independence and is empowered to investigate anyone, including members of the government, showcasing the importance of political will coupled with strong and independent institutions in combating corruption.

In Africa, Rwanda has made remarkable strides in fighting corruption, particularly noteworthy given the country's history of conflict and genocide. Rwanda's strategy has focused on strong leadership, political will, and the implementation of practical measures, such as the establishment of the Office of the Ombudsman and the National Public Procurement Authority. These institutions are tasked with promoting transparency, accountability, and integrity in public procurement processes, which are often prone to corruption. Rwanda's success highlights the significance of political commitment and the implementation of targeted reforms in sectors particularly vulnerable to corruption.

Comparing Australia's anti-corruption measures with these international examples reveals both strengths and areas for potential enhancement. Australia's robust legal framework, independent judiciary, and commitment to democratic principles provide a solid foundation for its anti-corruption efforts. However, the experiences of leading countries underscore the importance of ongoing innovation in anti-corruption strategies, the cultivation of a strong culture of transparency and integrity, and the need for continuous political commitment to anti-corruption efforts.

IMPROVE FREEDOM OF INFORMATION LEGISLATIONS AND ACCESS

Strengthening freedom of information laws in Australia is a pivotal aspect of reforming the political landscape to enhance government transparency. This requires a multifaceted approach that includes reviewing and amending existing legislation, reducing barriers to access, ensuring timely responses, and increasing proactive disclosure by government entities. Strengthening review and appeal processes, promoting a culture of openness within the government, leveraging technology, and boosting public awareness about FOI rights are also essential steps. By implementing these measures, Australia can improve public access to information, thereby fostering greater accountability, transparency, and trust in government operations.

REVIEW AND AMEND EXISTING LEGISLATION

Australia's Freedom of Information legislation plays a central role in promoting transparency and accountability within government operations, allowing the public unprecedented access to government-held information. This legislative framework is foundational to the democratic process, as it empowers citizens to participate more fully in their governance by scrutinising government actions and decisions. However, despite its significant benefits, the current state of FOI legislation in Australia faces challenges that limit its effectiveness and potential for fostering an open government.

At the core of FOI, it enhances public trust in governmental institutions by making the actions and decisions of public officials more visible and subject to public scrutiny. This visibility helps deter corrupt or unethical behaviour, as government officials are aware that their actions can be reviewed by the public. FOI legislation supports a more informed citizenry, which is crucial for the healthy functioning of a democracy. By facilitating access to information, individuals and organisations can contribute to more meaningful public debates and policy discussions. In addition, FOI acts as a mechanism for greater accountability, enabling citizens to seek redress or clarification on decisions impacting their lives and communities.

Despite these advantages, the current FOI framework in Australia encounters several problems that undermine its objectives. One of the most pressing issues is the legislation's provisions for secrecy and exemptions—at the behest of the government of the day and substantially undermines the intention of FOI—which are often criticised for being overly broad or for allowing too much discretion in withholding information. These provisions can lead to a culture of excessive secrecy, where information that should rightly be available to the public is unnecessarily classified as exempt. This not only erodes trust in public institutions but also hampers the public's ability to engage fully and effectively in democratic processes.

The criteria for exemptions under the current FOI laws merit a thorough re-evaluation. Exemptions intended to protect national security and personal privacy are undoubtedly important; however, the application of these exemptions requires careful balance to ensure they are not used to withhold information that is in the public interest. There are concerns that the threshold for what constitutes "national security" or "privacy" reasons can sometimes be set too low, leading to an unwarranted restriction of access to information.

To address these challenges and improve the effectiveness of FOI legislation, a comprehensive review and amendment of existing laws are necessary. This review should aim to narrow the scope of exemptions and introduce clearer, more stringent criteria for withholding information. By doing so, the legislation would minimise unnecessary secrecy and ensure that exemptions are applied only when genuinely required. The review process should also involve public consultation to gather insights and concerns from a broad range of stakeholders, including civil society organisations, journalists, and the general public. Such an inclusive approach would not only enhance the legitimacy of the FOI framework but also ensure that it reflects the public's information needs and concerns.

Improving the FOI legislation should go hand in hand with efforts to foster a culture of openness within government institutions. This includes training for public officials on the importance of transparency and the public's right to information, as well as implementing policies that encourage proactive disclosure of information that is of public interest.

REDUCE COSTS AND SIMPLIFY PROCEDURES

Despite the noble intentions of FOI, the effectiveness of this legislation is often hampered by practical barriers that discourage individuals from exercising their rights. Among these barriers, the costs associated with FOI requests and the complexity of the request procedures stand out as significant deterrents. Addressing these issues is crucial for enhancing the accessibility of information and reinforcing the democratic principles that underpin the FOI legislation.

While there is no cost in accessing personal information, the cost of making other FOI requests is at the discretion of the relevant minister or the Office of the Australian Information Commissioner, and this can be a substantial obstacle for many individuals and organisations. Fees for processing FOI requests, although intended to offset some of the administrative costs, can dissuade people from seeking information, particularly when the outcome of the request is uncertain. This is especially problematic when the information sought is in the public interest.

Simplifying the FOI request process is equally important. The current procedures can be daunting, especially for those who are not familiar with the legal and bureaucratic language often associated with government documents. Simplification can be achieved by providing clear, user-friendly guidelines and templates for submitting requests. Ensuring that these resources are readily available online would also contribute to lowering the barrier to entry for potential requestors.

The adoption of digital technologies presents a significant opportunity to streamline the FOI process further. Developing a centralised online portal where individuals can submit, track, and review the status of their FOI requests would introduce a level of transparency and efficiency currently lacking. Such a platform could provide users with updates on their requests, estimated completion times, and direct lines of communication with the relevant FOI officers. Incorporating features that allow for the digital submission and retrieval of documents could also significantly reduce processing times and administrative costs.

The principle of proactive disclosure should be embraced more fully within the FOI framework. By systematically making information that is frequently requested or of public interest readily available online, the government can pre-empt FOI requests, further reducing costs and administrative burdens for both the public and the government itself.

In implementing these measures, it is essential to ensure that the efforts to reduce costs and simplify procedures do not compromise the quality and comprehensiveness of the information provided. The ultimate goal is to enhance the public's access to information, thereby strengthening the accountability and transparency of government operations.

ENHANCE TIMELINESS OF RESPONSES

Prolonged delays in processing FOI requests not only frustrate the requesters but can also diminish the relevance and impact of the information once it is released. Enhancing the promptness of these responses is thus essential for upholding the principles of open government and maintaining public trust in the FOI system. To achieve this, implementing and enforcing stricter timelines for government agencies' responses to FOI requests, along with introducing penalties or incentives for compliance, are practical steps that could significantly improve the current situation.

Stricter timelines would serve as a clear benchmark for both FOI officers and requesters, setting realistic expectations for the processing time of requests. Currently, while there are standard time frames in place, exceptions and extensions can sometimes lead to extended delays. By tightening these rules and minimising the allowable extensions, agencies would be encouraged to prioritise the efficient handling of FOI requests. This requires not only legislative changes but also a commitment to enhancing the internal processes and resources dedicated to FOI management within each agency.

The introduction of agency penalties for non-compliance with these timelines could act as a deterrent against unnecessary delays. Penalties might include financial fines for the agencies responsible for the delay, which could be used to fund the FOI processing infrastructure or to support transparency initiatives. However, imposing penalties must be approached with caution, ensuring that they do not inadvertently encourage agencies to rush decisions and potentially withhold information unjustly to avoid fines.

Conversely, introducing incentives for timely compliance presents a positive reinforcement approach. Incentives could range from public recognition of agencies that consistently meet or exceed FOI processing standards to additional funding or resources to support their transparency efforts. This not only rewards good practice but also encourages a culture of openness and efficiency within government bodies.

INCREASE PROACTIVE DISCLOSURE

The concept of proactive disclosure by government agencies would embody a transformative approach to transparency and accountability, shifting from a reactive model, where information is provided only upon request, to a more open stance, where significant volumes of data are made available to the public by default. This strategy, particularly in the context of more recent behaviours of the Australian government, offers a promising avenue to enhance public access to information, potentially reducing the reliance on formal FOI requests. If a government was mandated to release information that the public has a right to know, why would the public want to delve further into FOI? In addition, revisiting and reducing the 20-year cabinet secrecy rules could play a crucial role in this shift towards greater openness.

Proactive disclosure entails the regular publication of information that holds public interest, such as government contracts, spending reports, policy documents, and more. While some of this information is currently available through portals such as AusTender procurement information system, most of details are hidden from the public view, or granted an exemption through the catch-all of "commercial-in-confidence".

By making such information readily accessible, the government can pre-empt a significant portion of FOI requests, which often seek information that could easily be made available through proactive measures. This not only facilitates a more informed citizenry but also alleviates the administrative burden on government agencies tasked with processing FOI requests, leading to a more efficient allocation of public resources.

The practice of proactive disclosure aligns with the principles of good governance, enhancing the transparency of governmental operations and decision-making processes. It fosters a culture of trust between the government and the public, as transparency acts as a deterrent against corruption and inefficiency. When people can easily access information about how public funds are being used or how decisions are made, it increases government accountability and public engagement in the democratic process.

The issue of cabinet secrecy, with its current 20-year confidentiality rule, represents a significant barrier to transparency. While the protection of sensitive deliberations is often justified to preserve the integrity of the decision-making process, the lengthy period of secrecy is increasingly seen as excessive. Reducing this period could significantly enhance historical accountability and public understanding of key government decisions and policies. Such a move would signal a strong commitment to transparency, indicating that the government prioritises the public's right to know over the preservation of outdated confidentiality practices.

However, the transition towards increased proactive disclosure and reduced cabinet secrecy must be carefully managed. There are legitimate concerns regarding the protection of sensitive information, particularly in areas related to national security, personal privacy, and commercial confidentiality. Therefore, any move towards greater openness must be balanced with adequate safeguards to protect these interests. Implementing clear guidelines on what constitutes public interest information and establishing robust processes for redacting sensitive data can help manage these concerns. This shift towards openness not only benefits the public but also enhances the legitimacy and effectiveness of the government itself, building a stronger, more engaged society.

HOW DOES AUSTRALIA'S FREEDOM OF INFORMATION COMPARE WITH INTERNATIONAL EXPERIENCES?

FOI systems around the globe vary significantly, reflecting the diverse legal, cultural, and political contexts within which they operate. However, some nations stand out for their exemplary FOI frameworks, offering valuable insights and best practices from which Australia could learn. By examining the characteristics that make these systems effective, Australia can identify opportunities to refine and enhance its own FOI framework, ensuring it remains responsive to the needs of its citizens and continues to uphold the principles of transparency and accountability.

One of the most lauded FOI systems is found in Sweden, home to the world's oldest freedom of information legislation, the *Freedom of the Press Act* of 1766. Sweden's system is characterised by its presumption in favour of access, where all government documents are automatically considered public unless explicitly exempted. This proactive stance towards information disclosure sets a high standard for transparency and simplifies the process for requesting information. Australia could adopt a similar presumption of openness, reducing the burden on requesters to justify the public interest in disclosure and encouraging a culture of transparency within government agencies.

Another noteworthy example is Estonia, renowned for its digital governance initiatives. Estonia's e-Government system enables citizens to access a wide array of government information online effortlessly. The integration of digital technologies has made Estonia's FOI system highly accessible and efficient, reducing the need for formal requests by making information readily available. Australia could look to Estonia's model for inspiration in leveraging technology to enhance its FOI system, particularly through the development of centralised online platforms for submitting FOI requests and accessing information.

The United Kingdom's FOI system also offers valuable lessons, particularly in terms of its independent oversight mechanism. The UK's Information Commissioner's Office plays a crucial role in enforcing FOI legislation, offering a free and accessible avenue for appealing government decisions on information requests. The ICO has the authority to order the release of information and can impose penalties for non-compliance, ensuring agencies take their FOI obligations seriously. Establishing or empowering a similar independent body in Australia could strengthen the enforcement of FOI rights and provide an effective recourse for individuals dissatisfied with government responses to their requests.

Norway presents another worthwhile model, especially in terms of proactive disclosure. Norwegian law requires government agencies to maintain public registers of their documents and to make these registers easily accessible to the public. This approach not only facilitates access to information but also reduces the administrative burden on agencies by diminishing the volume of individual requests. Adopting similar requirements for proactive disclosure and public registers in Australia could enhance transparency and improve the efficiency of the FOI process.

From these examples, several key themes emerge that could guide improvements to Australia's FOI system. The presumption of openness, as demonstrated by Sweden, encourages transparency and reduces barriers to access. Estonia's integration of digital technologies highlights the potential for e-Government solutions to streamline FOI processes. The UK's independent oversight mechanism underscores the importance of robust enforcement and appeal options. Lastly, Norway's proactive disclosure practices illustrate how making information readily available can benefit both the public and government agencies.

Incorporating these lessons into Australia's FOI framework requires a multifaceted approach, involving legislative reforms, technological investments, and cultural shifts within government agencies. By embracing the principles of openness, leveraging technology, ensuring independent oversight, and enhancing proactive disclosure, Australia can strengthen its FOI system, making it more accessible, efficient, and effective in serving the public interest. These reforms not only align with global best practices but could also reaffirm Australia's commitment to the foundational democratic values of transparency and accountability.

IMPLEMENT PROTECTION FOR WHISTLEBLOWERS AND PUBLIC INFORMANTS

To reform and improve Australian politics, it is imperative to enhance whistleblower protections significantly. By reviewing and amending existing laws, ensuring anonymity, establishing an independent agency for whistleblowers, and providing comprehensive support and remedies, Australia can create a safer environment for whistleblowers. Raising public awareness, implementing regular training, expanding the scope of protected disclosures, and establishing monitoring mechanisms are also essential steps. Such reforms will encourage the reporting of unethical behaviour, leading to greater accountability and transparency within both the public and private sectors, ultimately strengthening the integrity of Australian institutions.

COMPREHENSIVE REVIEW OF LEGISLATION

The importance of robust whistleblower protections cannot be overstated in the context of fostering an environment conducive to transparency and accountability, especially within the realms of governance and corporate conduct. In Australia, the necessity for strengthening these protections has become increasingly evident, underscored by high-profile cases such as those of "Witness K", David McBride, Richard Boyle and, although more relevant in an international context, Julian Assange. These instances not only illuminate the deficiencies in the current framework but also serve as a clarion call for a comprehensive legislative overhaul to safeguard those who expose wrongdoing.

Whistleblowers play a pivotal role in uncovering corruption, fraud, and other unethical behaviours, often at great personal risk. Their courage can lead to the revelation of information crucial for the public interest, driving reforms and ensuring accountability. However, the effectiveness of whistleblower and public informant protections in Australia is questionable, revealing a landscape where individuals face significant challenges in coming forward with information about wrongdoing due to fear of reprisal, litigation, and other forms of retribution.

A comprehensive review of existing whistleblower protection laws is essential to identify and address these gaps and weaknesses. This review should be rigorous and encompass a comparison with international best practices, drawing lessons from jurisdictions that have established more effective frameworks for whistleblower protection. Countries such as the United States, with its *Whistleblower Protection Act*, and member states of the European Union, which recently adopted a directive offering broad protections for whistleblowers, provide valuable benchmarks. These examples highlight the importance of ensuring anonymity, protecting against retaliation, and offering legal and financial support to whistleblowers.

The deficiencies in Australia's current system are numerous, including inadequate legal protections that leave whistleblowers vulnerable to legal action, professional retribution and imprisonment. Many individuals who have exposed wrongdoing have faced significant legal challenges, often coupled with a lack of financial and psychological support. This situation not only places immense strain on the individuals involved but also serves as a deterrent to potential whistleblowers, undermining efforts to promote a culture of openness and accountability.

To address these challenges, Australia must undertake a holistic reform of its whistleblower protection laws. While it was anticipated that such protections would be developed at part of the creation of the National Anti Corruption Commission, the Albanese government failed to take up this opportunity. Such protections could include creating mechanisms for anonymous reporting to protect the identity of whistleblowers and establishing clear, accessible channels for disclosures. Legal protections need to be bolstered to prevent retaliation against whistleblowers, with specific provisions to shield them from unfair dismissal, demotion, and other forms of professional punishment. The provision of financial assistance and legal aid is crucial to ensure that whistleblowers can defend themselves against any legal actions stemming from their disclosures.

The path forward requires not only legal reforms but a cultural shift towards recognising and valuing the critical role whistleblowers play in upholding integrity within both the public and private sectors.

ROBUST LEGAL PROTECTIONS AND SAFEGUARDS OF ANONYMITY

Amending legislation to include robust legal protections and anonymity safeguards is essential and these amendments would not only align Australia's approach with international best practices but also signal a firm commitment to upholding the principles of transparency and integrity within both the public and private sectors.

Firstly, providing comprehensive legal protections for whistleblowers is crucial. This entails safeguarding individuals who report misconduct in good faith from criminal charges, civil liability, and employment-related retaliation. Such protections should be clearly articulated in legislation, offering whistleblowers a solid legal foundation upon which to stand when they make the difficult decision to come forward. For instance, amendments could include provisions that explicitly prohibit the initiation of criminal proceedings against whistleblowers for disclosing information about misconduct, provided the disclosure was made in good faith and with a reasonable belief in its truthfulness.

Protection from civil liability is equally important, as whistleblowers can often be deterred by the threat of costly legal battles, even if they ultimately prevail. Legislation should, therefore, include provisions that immunise whistleblowers from lawsuits related to their disclosures, again, provided that these disclosures are made in good faith and are not knowingly false. This legal shield would significantly lower the barriers to reporting wrongdoing, encouraging more individuals to come forward.

Employment-related retaliation is another area where whistleblowers require robust protections. Amendments to Australian legislation should ensure that individuals who report misconduct are safeguarded against any form of workplace retaliation, including termination, demotion, harassment, or any other adverse employment action. Such provisions could also introduce mandatory remedies for retaliatory actions, such as reinstatement, compensation for lost wages, and damages for emotional distress. Additionally, establishing a presumption in favour of the whistleblower in disputes about retaliatory actions could shift the burden of proof to the employer to demonstrate that any adverse action was not related to the employee's disclosure.

By providing a safe and secure environment for whistleblowers, Australia can significantly improve its transparency and governance, reinforcing the public's trust in its institutions.

AN INDEPENDENT WHISTLEBLOWER AGENCY

The establishment of an independent whistleblower or public informant agency could represents a critical advancement in bolstering transparency, accountability, and ethical conduct within Australia's public and private sectors. This proposed entity would serve as a cornerstone for whistleblower protection, offering a centralised and authoritative resource dedicated to the support and advocacy of individuals exposing misconduct. The creation of such an agency underscores a commitment to fostering an environment where whistleblowers are not only protected but valued for their contribution to integrity and accountability.

The agency, which could be named the Public Advocate or Public Informant Agency, would perform multiple critical functions. Firstly, it would offer a secure and confidential channel for whistleblowers to report misconduct, ensuring that individuals can come forward without fear of reprisal. This would involve the development and maintenance of secure reporting mechanisms, such as encrypted digital platforms, confidential hotlines, and safe mail drops, catering to the diverse needs and circumstances of potential whistleblowers.

Secondly, the agency would play a crucial advisory role, providing whistleblowers with guidance on the reporting process, their rights, and the protections available to them under Australian law. This could include offering legal advice, counseling services, and support navigating the complexities that often accompany the decision to blow the whistle on unethical practices. By demystifying the process and offering tangible support, the agency would empower more individuals to take a stand against misconduct.

A critical aspect of the agency's role would be its enforcement powers. To effectively protect whistleblowers and hold retaliators accountable, the agency would need the legal authority to impose sanctions or seek remedies for those who suffer from retaliation. This could range from financial penalties for individuals or entities found to be in violation of whistleblower protection laws, to advocating for compensatory measures for affected whistleblowers, such as reinstatement or compensation for lost income and emotional distress.

For such an agency to function effectively, it must operate with a high degree of independence from governmental or corporate influence. This independence is crucial to ensure that the agency can carry out its duties without bias or interference. The establishment of the Public Advocate or Public Informant Agency could be underpinned by legislation that clearly delineates its powers, functions, and governance structure, ensuring its autonomy and its alignment with the principles of transparency and justice.

Such an agency would not only safeguard individuals who act in the public interest but also contribute to the detection and correction of misconduct that undermines the integrity of Australian institutions and would mark a significant milestone in Australia's ongoing efforts to foster a culture of openness, integrity, and accountability.

SUPPORT AND REMEDIATION FOR WHISTLEBLOWERS

The plight of whistleblowers like David McBride (providing documents that contained information about war crimes committed by Australian soldiers in Afghanistan), Bernard Collaery (releasing material about the Australian governments bugging of the Timor-Leste cabinet offices), and Richard Boyle (exposed abuse of power within the Australian Taxation Office), whose lives have been profoundly impacted by their courageous decisions to expose wrongdoing, underscores a critical vulnerability in Australia's approach to whistleblower protection.

These individuals, having acted in the public interest, faced severe repercussions that not only disrupted their professional careers but also had far-reaching effects on their personal lives and wellbeing. This situation brings to light the essential need for comprehensive support and remediation for whistleblowers, as well as the role of regular training and public awareness in creating a protective environment for those who come forward with information on unethical behavior.

Public awareness campaigns can further reinforce the value of whistleblowing in promoting accountability and ethical conduct. By elevating the public perception of whistleblowers and educating the community about their rights and protections, these campaigns can help to dismantle the stigma often associated with whistleblowing. Increased awareness among the general public can also lead to greater support for whistleblowers, providing an additional layer of protection against retaliation and ostracism.

By prioritising the protection and support of whistleblowers, Australia can strengthen its commitment to transparency, accountability, and ethical governance, ensuring that the sacrifices made by whistleblowers do not go unrecognised or unrewarded.

PROTECTION FOR A BROAD RANGE OF DISCLOSURES

The breadth of issues that could necessitate whistleblower disclosures is vast, underscoring the need for protections that encompass a wide range of unethical or illegal activities. This comprehensive scope is essential in fostering an environment where individuals feel empowered and protected to report misconduct without fear of retribution.

Whistleblower protections must be broad and inclusive, covering various forms of misconduct that can impact the organization, its stakeholders, and the wider community. This includes, but is not limited to, corruption, which undermines trust and integrity within both public and private institutions. Financial malfeasance, encompassing fraud, embezzlement, and other forms of financial impropriety, represents another critical area. Such activities not only affect the financial health of organisations but also erode investor confidence and can have severe economic repercussions.

Public health risks form another vital category. In the context of increasing global interconnectedness and the potential for widespread impact, disclosures related to unsafe practices, hazardous conditions, or other threats to public health are of paramount importance. The COVID-19 pandemic has highlighted the critical role whistleblowers can play in early detection and response to emerging health crises, underscoring the need for protections that encourage the reporting of such risks.

Violations of human rights are yet another domain where whistleblower disclosures can be crucial. This encompasses a broad spectrum of issues, including workplace discrimination, harassment, exploitation, and abuses of power that infringe upon individuals' rights and dignity. In many cases, these violations may be systemic, hidden from public view, and deeply entrenched within organisational cultures, making the role of whistleblowers particularly significant in bringing them to light.

The scope of whistleblower protections in Australia must be comprehensive, covering a broad array of unethical and illegal behaviours. By ensuring that protections are clear, inclusive, and supported by both legal frameworks and organisational cultures, Australia can enhance its capacity to address misconduct effectively.

INTERNATIONAL AGENCIES

As is the case in anti-corruption measures and freedom of access to government information, there are several countries have set compelling precedents in the establishment of robust whistleblower protection frameworks and agencies. These international models exemplify best practices in safeguarding whistleblowers from retaliation, ensuring their concerns are addressed, and fostering a culture of transparency and accountability. Australia, in its quest to refine and strengthen its own whistleblower protections, can draw valuable insights from these global benchmarks.

One of the standout examples is the United States, which has a comprehensive framework for whistleblower protection across various sectors. The *Whistleblower Protection Act* primarily covers federal employees, protecting them from retaliation for disclosing government illegality, waste, and corruption. In addition, the *Dodd-Frank Wall Street Reform and Consumer Protection Act* offers protections and incentives for whistleblowers in the financial services sector, including monetary rewards for those whose information leads to successful legal actions. The United States also has the Office of the Whistleblower under the Securities and Exchange Commission, which is tasked with handling tips, complaints, and referrals of securities law violations. This structured approach ensures that whistleblowers have clear avenues for disclosure and protection, a model that could be adapted to Australia's context to cover various sectors with specific nuances.

In the European Union, the Directive on the Protection of Persons Who Report Breaches of Union Law, adopted in 2019, marks a significant step forward in unifying whistleblower protections across member states. This directive mandates that all EU countries establish secure channels for internal and external reporting, along with measures to protect whistleblowers from retaliation. It covers a wide range of EU laws, including those related to financial services, money laundering, public procurement, and environmental protection. The directive emphasises the importance of providing clear reporting channels, feedback mechanisms for whistleblowers, and a comprehensive approach to protection that could serve as a model for Australian reforms.

Scandinavia, particularly Norway, is renowned for its high levels of transparency and public trust in government, partly due to its effective whistleblower protections. Norway's *Working Environment Act* provides extensive protections for employees who report on unethical practices, ensuring anonymity and protection against retaliation. Furthermore, the Norwegian Labour Inspection Authority plays a crucial role in overseeing and enforcing these protections, offering a governmental model that actively supports and safeguards whistleblowers.

New Zealand offers another exemplary model with its *Protected Disclosures (Protection of Whistleblowers) Act 2020*, which strengthens the legal protections for whistleblowers, making it easier for them to report misconduct. The Act requires public sector organisations to provide support for whistleblowers and establishes clear procedures for handling disclosures. This approach of mandating organisational support and clear procedural guidelines could be particularly relevant for Australia, ensuring that whistleblowers are not only protected but also supported throughout the reporting process.

Drawing from these international examples, several key themes emerge that could guide Australia in enhancing its whistleblower protections and frameworks. First, the importance of establishing clear, accessible, and secure reporting channels cannot be overstated. Whether through dedicated agencies like the SEC's Office of the Whistleblower or through legislative mandates as seen in the EU and New Zealand, ensuring that whistleblowers can easily and safely report misconduct is crucial.

Second, providing comprehensive protections against retaliation is essential. This includes legal safeguards, as well as support mechanisms to assist whistleblowers through potential challenges arising from their disclosures. The examples of the United States and Norway highlight the effectiveness of combining legal protections with active oversight and enforcement mechanisms.

Lastly, incentivising whistleblowing through rewards or acknowledgments, as seen in the Dodd-Frank Act, can be a powerful tool in encouraging the disclosure of wrongdoing. While such measures must be carefully designed to avoid unintended consequences, they can significantly enhance the effectiveness of whistleblower frameworks.

Incorporating these elements into Australia's approach to whistleblower protection could significantly strengthen the system, fostering an environment where whistleblowers are supported, protected, and valued for their critical role in upholding integrity and accountability.

*

CHAPTER 4: POLITICAL PARTY AND GOVERNANCE REFORMS

INTRODUCE TERM LIMITS

Incorporating term limits for politicians in Australia could serve as a rejuvenating force in politics, encouraging innovation, accountability, and a more dynamic and representative democracy. However, the success of such a measure depends on its thoughtful implementation, taking into account the lessons learned from international examples and the unique context of Australian politics.

ENCOURAGEMENT OF NEW IDEAS AND LEADERSHIP

In the discourse on political renewal and the infusion of innovative thinking into the legislative process, the concept of imposing term limits on parliamentary members in Australia presents a compelling avenue for exploration. The advocacy for such a reform is grounded in the belief that it could significantly enhance the dynamism and responsiveness of political leadership, while concurrently amplifying the diversity of voices and perspectives within the halls of governance.

At the heart of this proposition is the notion that fresh perspectives are indispensable for the vitality of democratic deliberation and policy-making. The imposition of term limits is seen as a mechanism to guarantee a perpetual infusion of new leaders into the political arena. These individuals, untethered from the inertia that can accompany prolonged tenure in office, are more likely to bring innovative ideas and fresh approaches to addressing the multifaceted challenges that contemporary society faces. This continuous renewal of leadership is not merely about changing faces but is fundamentally about injecting new ways of thinking and problem-solving into the political discourse. It is about ensuring that the political class evolves in tandem with the society it aims to serve, reflecting its evolving needs, aspirations, and challenges.

The introduction of term limits holds the promise of fostering a more diverse and representative political landscape. In the absence of entrenched incumbency, the barriers to entry for underrepresented groups—be it on the basis of ethnicity, gender, socioeconomic background, or professional experience—could be significantly lowered. This democratisation of political participation would not only enrich the policy debate with a wider array of perspectives but also enhance the legitimacy and responsiveness of the political system. When leadership is more reflective of the society's demographic and ideological diversity, the policies and initiatives it champions are more likely to resonate with the broader populace, fostering a sense of inclusivity and collective ownership over the political process.

The careers of long-serving politicians such as Prime Minister Anthony Albanese and Leader of the Opposition Peter Dutton illustrate a broader systemic issue within the Australian political landscape—the phenomenon of political institutionalisation. With Albanese's 28 years and Dutton's 24 years of service in parliament, politicians with extended tenures can become too entrenched within the system, potentially leading to a scenario where the focus shifts from public service, to the preservation of one's position within the political hierarchy. This entrenchment can stifle innovation and deter meaningful engagement with novel ideas and approaches. The argument for term limits hinges on the belief that by curbing the potential for politicians to become institutionalised, the political arena can be made more dynamic and open to individuals who are motivated by the desire to effect change rather than the pursuit of a career in politics. This, in turn, could mitigate the cynicism that often surrounds political figures and reinvigorate public trust and interest in the democratic process.

Term limits, could be a transformative reform that could recalibrate the focus of political engagement towards the pursuit of innovation, inclusivity, and responsive governance. By ensuring that political leadership is continually refreshed, the system becomes inherently more adaptable and reflective of contemporary societal dynamics. This reform is not without its challenges and detractors, who might argue about the loss of experienced leadership and the nuances of implementing such a system. However, the potential benefits—a more vibrant, diverse, and forward-thinking body politic—present a compelling case for considering term limits as a catalyst for the renewal of political leadership and the enrichment of democratic governance in Australia.

PREVENTION OF POWER ENTRENCHMENT

The core rationale for instituting term limits is the prevention of power entrenchment. Power, when held unchecked for prolonged durations, can foster an environment ripe for corruption and diminish the accountability mechanisms essential to democratic governance. Term limits serve as a direct countermeasure to this threat, imposing a predefined boundary to the tenure of officeholders. This limitation compels a cyclical renewal of leadership, thereby preventing any single individual or group from embedding themselves within the fabric of the political establishment to an extent that they become insurmountable. It's a principle aimed at ensuring that the corridors of power are not closed corridors but are instead pathways open to new entrants, thereby preserving the dynamism and responsiveness of the political system.

The introduction of term limits could also be viewed as an effective strategy to dismantle political monopolies and deter the formation of political dynasties. Such dynasties, where political influence and office are passed down through familial or close network lines, can lead to a monopolisation of political opportunities, where the prospect of electoral success becomes heavily skewed in favour of established political names and networks. This monopolisation not only restricts the diversity of political representation but also entrenches existing power structures, making it increasingly challenging for new voices and perspectives to gain a foothold in the political arena. By enforcing term limits, the cycle that perpetuates political dynasties can be broken, facilitating a more democratic and equitable distribution of political power. Term limits can act as a democratising force, ensuring that political office remains accessible to a broader cross-section of society, rather than being the preserve of a select few.

The concept of term limits as a preventative measure against the entrenchment of power is rooted in the recognition of the inherent dangers posed by static leadership. Such dangers include not only the potential for corrupt practices to become entrenched but also the risk of creating a political class that is increasingly disconnected from the electorate. In a system where political longevity is unchecked, there is a tendency for leaders to become insulated within a bubble of power, losing touch with the evolving needs and concerns of the populace. Term limits, by mandating a turnover of local representation and political leadership, ensure that those in positions of power remain grounded and attuned to the society they serve, reinforcing the accountability and representativeness of the political system.

INTERNATIONAL SUCCESS STORIES

The implementation of term limits has been a subject of considerable debate across the globe, with various nations adopting distinct approaches to the concept. The rationale behind these measures often revolves around the desire to promote democratic renewal and prevent the concentration of power. International experiences with term limits provide valuable insights into their effectiveness and the diverse ways they can be structured to achieve political rejuvenation and ensure a dynamic leadership landscape. Notably, the United States and several countries in Latin America serve as illustrative examples of how term limits can be successfully integrated into the political framework to foster a balance between experience and innovation.

In the United States, the adoption of the 22nd Amendment to the Constitution, which imposes a two-term limit on the presidency, stands as a central example of how terms can be limited. This amendment, ratified in 1951, was largely a reaction to Franklin D. Roosevelt's unprecedented four-term tenure, which had sparked concerns over the potential for executive power to become overly dominant. The two-term limit is widely regarded as a mechanism that has contributed significantly to the vibrancy and renewal of American democracy and by ensuring that no individual can hold the office of President for more than two terms, the system promotes regular infusion of new leadership into the highest echelon of government. This turnover at the apex of political power not only prevents the ossification of leadership but also encourages a broad spectrum of candidates to aspire to the presidency, enhancing the democratic process by providing voters with diverse choices and fresh perspectives.

In Latin America, a region known for its dynamic and often tumultuous political experiences, the approach to term limits has varied, with some countries experimenting with non-consecutive term limits. This model allows politicians to serve multiple terms in office but requires them to step down after a certain period before they can run for election again. This system aims to strike a balance between leveraging the experience of seasoned politicians and injecting new blood into the political arena. Countries like Chile and Brazil have implemented variations of this system, reflecting a nuanced understanding of the need for both continuity and change in leadership. The non-consecutive term limit model recognises the value of experience and the benefits of renewal, allowing former leaders to bring their knowledge back to the political forefront after a hiatus, during which time other leaders have had the opportunity to govern and introduce new ideas.

The international success stories of term limits underscore the principle that effective governance requires a delicate balance between continuity and change. The American and Latin American experiences highlight the adaptability of term limits as a concept, tailored to fit the unique political and cultural contexts of different countries. In the United States, the two-term limit for the presidency has become a cornerstone of the political system, ensuring regular leadership renewal at the highest level. In contrast, the flexible approach in Latin America, with non-consecutive term limits, offers a model that accommodates the return of experienced leaders while still fostering periodic leadership refreshment.

These examples serve as compelling evidence of term limits' potential to enhance democratic governance by preventing the entrenchment of power and promoting a healthy turnover in political leadership. The success of term limits in these contexts suggests that, when thoughtfully implemented, they can contribute significantly to the vibrancy and responsiveness of democratic systems, ensuring that leadership remains dynamic, representative, and attuned to the evolving needs of the populace.

DEBATE ON THE IDEAL TERM LENGTH

The consideration of reasonable term limits is underpinned by the recognition that effective governance requires both stability and dynamism. On one hand, the enactment of meaningful, impactful policies often necessitates a horizon that extends beyond the immediate electoral cycle, allowing for the careful planning, execution, and assessment of legislative and policy initiatives. On the other hand, the vitality of a democracy is sustained by its capacity for renewal, ensuring that its leaders remain responsive and attuned to the evolving needs and aspirations of the society they serve.

In this context, the proposal of a three-term limit for parliamentary positions in Australia emerges as a point of convergence between these two considerations. A three-term limit, assuming the current duration of terms in the Australian Federal Parliament, would provide an individual with up to twelve years in office. This span is considered sufficient for politicians to articulate their vision, navigate the legislative process, oversee the implementation of their policies, and witness the initial impacts of their governance decisions. It offers a temporal framework that respects the complexity and scale of governmental responsibilities, acknowledging that profound, systemic change often unfolds over extended periods.

Simultaneously, a three-term limit acts as a safeguard against the entrenchment of political power. By setting a definitive endpoint to the tenure of officeholders, it introduces a mechanism for regular, mandated political renewal. This limit compels political parties to cultivate a broader base of potential leaders, reducing the risk of overreliance on a small cadre of individuals and thereby diversifying the pool of expertise and perspectives within the political arena. It also mitigates the risk of politicians becoming too insulated or detached from the constituencies they represent, as the knowledge that their tenure is finite incentivises ongoing engagement and responsiveness to the public will.

The principle of flexibility and adaptability in the application of term limits acknowledges the diverse nature of political roles within the Australian system. The roles of a backbencher, a minister, or the prime minister, for instance, come with different responsibilities, scopes of influence, and public profiles. Therefore, while a uniform term limit provides a clear framework for political renewal, the application of this principle may need to be nuanced to accommodate the distinct characteristics of various offices. This might involve considerations of whether certain leadership positions, particularly those requiring extensive expertise or international negotiation skills, should be granted exceptions or modified term limits.

IMPLEMENTATION CHALLENGES AND CONSIDERATIONS

The introduction of term limits in Australia, while offering a promising avenue for political renewal and preventing the entrenchment of power, comes with its own set of challenges and considerations that necessitate careful deliberation. The venture into reforming the structure of political tenure is not merely about altering the rules of engagement for elected officials; it fundamentally touches upon the dynamics of governance, the cultivation of leadership, and the integrity of democratic processes. As such, the implementation of term limits must be approached with a nuanced understanding of its potential impacts, both intended and unintended, and a strategic plan to navigate the transition.

One of the foremost challenges in implementing term limits is the management of transition periods. This aspect is critical, as it concerns the immediate practicality of integrating the new system within the existing political landscape. For current officeholders, the introduction of term limits necessitates the establishment of transitional provisions that are both fair and conducive to maintaining stability in governance. These provisions would need to be carefully calibrated to ensure that they do not inadvertently disadvantage or unfairly advantage current politicians, thereby maintaining the reform's credibility and impartiality. The transition plan must also consider the timing of implementation to avoid disrupting the legislative cycle or causing undue political instability.

Another significant challenge is the potential for unintended consequences, a concern that underscores the complexity of political ecosystems and the interconnectivity of its various components. One of the primary apprehensions is the loss of experienced leaders. While term limits are designed to foster renewal and prevent the monopolisation of power, they also mean that individuals who have accumulated a wealth of knowledge and expertise over years of service would have to vacate their positions. This loss of institutional memory and the departure of skilled policymakers could create a vacuum that might not be easily or immediately filled by incoming officials, potentially leading to a dilution in the quality of governance, at least in the short term.

In addition, the vacuum created by the departure of seasoned politicians could inadvertently empower unelected officials and lobbyists. In scenarios where experienced legislators are replaced by less experienced ones, there is a risk that the actual crafting and shaping of policy could shift towards the bureaucracy and lobbying entities. These groups, not subject to term limits, might gain undue influence over the legislative process, as new lawmakers might rely more heavily on their expertise and networks. This shift could alter the balance of power within the political system, raising questions about accountability and the democratic principle that elected representatives should have the primary role in decision-making.

The implementation of term limits could also catalyse changes in the political culture, with both positive and negative implications. On the one hand, the prospect of term limits might encourage a more results-oriented approach among politicians, knowing that their time in office is finite. On the other hand, it could also lead to short-termism, with officeholders focusing on policies that yield immediate benefits, potentially at the expense of long-term planning and sustainability.

Taking these factors into account, the introduction of term limits is not a panacea for all the challenges facing the political system but represents a significant shift that could bring about substantial benefits as well as pose considerable risks. The success of such a reform depends on the careful consideration of these challenges and the development of strategies to mitigate potential downsides. This includes crafting thoughtful transition provisions, developing programs to rapidly upskill new politicians, ensuring mechanisms are in place to preserve institutional memory, and maintaining a vigilant eye on the influence of unelected entities. Ultimately, the goal is to enhance the dynamism, responsiveness, and accountability of Australia's political system, ensuring it remains robust and representative of the people it serves.

STRENGTHEN PARLIAMENTARY COMMITTEES

Strengthening the roles of parliamentary committees in Australia, through enhanced independence and the innovative use of both lay and expert committees, holds the potential to significantly improve the legislative process. This approach could lead to more informed policymaking, greater accountability, and a deeper connection between the public and the legislative process. However, success would hinge on careful implementation, including provisions for independence, resources, and balanced representation of expertise and public perspective.

ENHANCED OVERSIGHT AND INDEPENDENCE

With the system of democratic governance, parliamentary committees stand as pillars of oversight and accountability, providing a crucial mechanism for the scrutiny of government actions and policies. In Australia, enhancing and strengthening these committees is increasingly recognised as essential for deepening the democratic process and ensuring that governance is conducted in the public interest. The imperative to bolster the role and independence of these committees is driven by the dual goals of increasing accountability and enabling specialised scrutiny of government functions.

The potential of parliamentary committees to enhance accountability lies in their capacity to conduct detailed investigations and inquiries into the conduct of government and the implementation of policy. By strengthening these bodies, there is an opportunity to foster a more transparent political environment where decisions and policies are made openly, and public officials are held to account for their actions. This increased accountability is not merely about exposing wrongdoing or inefficiency; it is fundamentally about reinforcing the trust between the electorate and their representatives. When committees are empowered to effectively oversee government activities, they act as a conduit for public scrutiny, ensuring that elected officials and public servants operate not only within the bounds of legality but also in alignment with the expectations and interests of the public they serve.

The specialised nature of parliamentary committees also allows for a level of scrutiny that is often unattainable within the broader, more general debates that take place in the legislative chambers. By concentrating on specific policy areas or issues, committees can delve deeply into subjects, drawing on expert testimony and detailed evidence to assess the efficacy and impact of government policies and initiatives. This specialised scrutiny is particularly crucial in an era marked by the increasing complexity of social, economic, and environmental challenges. Committees, through their focused inquiries, can parse the intricacies of these issues, providing nuanced insights and recommendations that contribute to more informed and effective policymaking. In this way, they complement the broader work of the parliament, adding depth and precision to the legislative oversight of government.

To realise the full potential of parliamentary committees in enhancing oversight and accountability, it is essential to ensure their independence. This independence is multi-faceted, encompassing not only the autonomy of committees from direct governmental control but also ensuring they have access to sufficient resources and possess the authority to conduct their inquiries effectively. Independence is the bedrock upon which the credibility and effectiveness of committee scrutiny rest. Without it, the ability of committees to function as instruments of accountability and venues for specialised examination is severely compromised. Ensuring the independence of committees involves both structural and procedural safeguards, from the method of selecting committee members to the processes governing how inquiries are initiated and conducted.

The strengthening of parliamentary committees in Australia represents a strategic investment in the health of its democracy. By enhancing the accountability and oversight capabilities of these committees, the government demonstrates a commitment to governance that is transparent, responsive, and informed. By enabling specialised scrutiny of complex policy areas, committees can also provide valuable insights that refine and improve the policymaking process. The challenge lies in crafting and implementing reforms that preserve the independence of committees and empower them to fulfill their critical role in the democratic system. In doing so, Australia can ensure that its parliamentary committees continue to serve as effective stewards of public interest, contributing to a more accountable, transparent, and effective governance.

EFFECTIVENESS OF PARLIAMENTARY COMMITTEES IN THE PAST

Parliamentary committees in Australia's political history presents a narrative of fluctuating fortunes, where the impact of these entities on policy and legislative development has oscillated between significant achievements and moments of constrained efficacy. This dichotomy reflects the complex interplay of factors that influence the function and influence of parliamentary committees within the broader legislative and governance process. The varied experiences of these committees over time highlight not only their potential as instruments of policy scrutiny and legislative refinement but also the challenges that can impede their effectiveness.

In periods where parliamentary committees have been accorded substantial independence and provided with adequate resources, they have demonstrated an impressive capacity to contribute to the development and refinement of policy and legislation. The independence of committees is a crucial factor that allows them to operate without undue influence from the executive branch, enabling a more objective and thorough examination of issues. This autonomy is complemented by adequate resourcing, which encompasses not only financial allocations but also access to expertise and information, facilitating comprehensive inquiries into complex policy areas. Under such conditions, committees have been central in conducting in-depth analyses, engaging a broad range of stakeholders, and generating detailed reports that have informed and influenced legislative processes and policy formulation. These instances underscore the potential of parliamentary committees to act as vital forums for evidence-based policy deliberation, contributing to more nuanced and effective legislative outcomes.

However, the journey of parliamentary committees has not been without its challenges. Partisan politics, limited resources, and constraints on their authority have periodically undermined their effectiveness. The intrusion of partisan considerations into the workings of committees can compromise their objectivity, leading to outcomes that reflect political priorities rather than evidence-based policy considerations. This politicisation can detract from the credibility of committees and diminish their role as impartial forums for policy scrutiny.

Limited resources have also been a persistent challenge, affecting the ability of committees to conduct thorough inquiries and engage with a wide range of expertise and perspectives. Financial constraints, limited access to independent expert advice, and insufficient staff support can hamper the depth and breadth of committee inquiries, limiting their ability to scrutinise complex policy issues comprehensively.

Constraints on the authority of committees represent another significant challenge, affecting their capacity to call witnesses, access documents, and conduct inquiries with the necessary depth and rigour. Without sufficient authority, committees may struggle to obtain the information and cooperation necessary to fulfill their mandate effectively, impacting their ability to hold the government and other entities to account.

Despite these challenges, the history of parliamentary committees in Australia has many examples of resilience and adaptation. Committees have, at times, navigated the constraints of partisan politics, resource limitations, and authority restrictions to deliver insights and recommendations that have shaped policy and legislation in meaningful ways. The mixed results of their endeavours reflect the dynamic and contested nature of political governance, highlighting the ongoing need to reinforce the independence, resourcing, and authority of parliamentary committees.

THE POTENTIAL OF LAY AND EXPERT COMMITTEES

The innovative concept of integrating both lay and expert committees into the politics of Australia presents a promising avenue for enhancing the democratic process, fostering greater public engagement, and elevating the quality of policy and legislative development. This dual approach to committee composition seeks to marry the rich, varied perspectives of the general public with the nuanced, specialised knowledge of experts, creating a more inclusive and informed legislative process.

Lay committees, which incorporate members of the public who may not have formal expertise in the matters under consideration, offer a novel means of democratising the oversight and policy formulation processes. By bringing in individuals from diverse backgrounds and experiences, these committees can ensure that a wider array of perspectives is considered in the deliberation of complex policy issues. This approach not only enriches the pool of ideas and considerations but also serves to ground policy discussions in the everyday realities and concerns of the populace. The involvement of lay members in the policy process can also enhance public understanding of and engagement with complex issues, bridging the gap between citizens and the often esoteric world of policy-making. Through this engagement, lay committees can foster a sense of ownership and investment among the public, contributing to a more vibrant and participatory democracy.

Expert committees, on the other hand, draw on the specialised knowledge and expertise of professionals and scholars to provide deep, technical insights into policy and legislative issues. Composed of specialists in relevant fields, these committees can offer detailed analyses and recommendations that are grounded in the latest research and best practices. The contributions of expert committees are invaluable in navigating the intricacies of complex policy areas, from healthcare and environment to finance and technology. By leveraging the depth of expertise available within these committees, the legislative process can benefit from a level of scrutiny and insight that significantly enhances the quality and effectiveness of policy outcomes.

The potential of a balanced approach that incorporates both lay and expert committees lies in its ability to harness the strengths of broad public engagement and specialised expertise. Such a system can ensure that policy development is both democratically grounded and intellectually rigorous, reflecting the lived experiences of the public while being shaped by the best available knowledge and analysis. This dual approach encourages a more holistic examination of policy issues, fostering outcomes that are both innovative and responsive to the needs and aspirations of society.

In Australia, experiments with deliberative democracy in the early 2000s provide a glimpse into the potential of engaging lay committees in the political process. Initiatives such as citizens' juries and deliberative polls invited randomly selected members of the public to deliberate on specific policy issues, offering recommendations that were informed by expert input yet rooted in the values and priorities of the community. These experiments demonstrated the feasibility and value of incorporating lay perspectives into the decision-making process, highlighting the potential for such approaches to enhance the legitimacy and responsiveness of governance.

INTERNATIONAL EXAMPLES

The international landscape offers a plethora of examples where parliamentary committees exert significant influence on policy scrutiny, legislative refinement, and the broader democratic process. Among these, the committee systems of the German Bundestag and the United Kingdom's Parliament stand out for their effectiveness, structure, and impact. These examples provide valuable insights into how committees can function as powerful instruments of democracy, contributing to informed policymaking and enhancing governmental accountability.

Germany's Bundestag operates a committee system that is widely recognised for its comprehensive approach to policy scrutiny. One of the system's most notable features is its blend of expert and lay input, which ensures that a wide range of perspectives is considered in the legislative process. This inclusive approach enriches the deliberations and contributes to more balanced and well-considered outcomes. The committees of the Bundestag also enjoy a significant degree of independence, which is crucial for their ability to conduct unbiased reviews of legislation and government actions. This independence is safeguarded by procedural rules and the composition of the committees, which reflect the proportionality of the political parties represented in the Bundestag. As a result, the committees are empowered to undertake rigorous investigations and provide critical oversight without undue influence from the executive branch. The effectiveness of the Bundestag's committee system is evidenced by its role in shaping major policy initiatives and its capacity to adapt and respond to emerging challenges, underscoring the value of combining diverse inputs and maintaining independence in legislative scrutiny.

The United Kingdom's parliamentary committees have carved a niche for themselves as critical entities in the landscape of governance and accountability. Known for their detailed investigations and impactful reports, these committees have a track record of influencing both policy decisions and public opinion. The strength of the UK's committee system lies in its relative independence and its ability to draw upon a wide range of expertise. Committees in the UK Parliament frequently call upon experts, stakeholders, and the public to contribute evidence and viewpoints, ensuring that their inquiries are informed by a comprehensive array of insights. This practice not only enhances the depth and quality of the committees' work but also fosters transparency and public engagement in the legislative process. The reports produced by these committees often receive considerable attention, shaping discourse around key issues and sometimes prompting significant policy shifts or governmental action. The success of the UK's parliamentary committees illustrates the potential of such bodies to serve as effective watchdogs and critical contributors to policy development when they operate with sufficient autonomy and access to expertise.

These international experiences offer valuable lessons for countries such as Australia looking to strengthen their own parliamentary committee systems, emphasising the importance of structure, independence, and inclusivity in achieving effective legislative oversight.

IMPLEMENTATION CONSIDERATIONS

In the endeavour to forge stronger and more efficacious parliamentary committees in Australia, a meticulous approach that encompasses both structural reforms and enhanced support mechanisms is essential. This dual focus aims not only to elevate the stature and operational capacity of these committees but also to ensure they can function as instruments for legislative oversight, policy scrutiny, and public engagement. The aspiration to refine the Australian parliamentary committee system invites a thoughtful consideration of the frameworks and supports necessary to realise these objectives.

Structural reforms stand at the forefront of this initiative, addressing the foundational elements that govern the composition, authority, and operational dynamics of parliamentary committees. One of the primary considerations in this domain is the augmentation of the committees' authority. Empowering committees with greater investigative powers, such as the ability to summon witnesses and access documents, would enhance their ability to conduct thorough inquiries and hold government agencies and officials to account. Ensuring the independence of these committees from executive influence is also crucial. This might involve reforms to the appointment processes for committee members, aiming to safeguard against partisan considerations and promote a composition that mirrors the diversity and balance of the parliament itself.

The provision of adequate resources is also indispensable for the effectiveness of parliamentary committees. This encompasses financial allocations sufficient to cover in-depth research, stakeholder consultations, and the dissemination of findings.

It also involves access to expert advisors and analysts who can support the committees in navigating complex policy areas and interpreting technical information. Ensuring that committees are well-resourced is fundamental to enabling them to fulfill their mandate of scrutinising legislation and policy with the requisite depth and rigour.

In tandem with structural reforms, the implementation considerations must also encompass the training and support of committee members. For lay members, who bring valuable non-expert perspectives to the deliberation process, targeted training can enhance their understanding of legislative procedures, policy analysis, and evidence evaluation. This support is vital for maximising the contributions of lay members, enabling them to engage meaningfully with complex issues and bridging the gap between public sentiment and policy discourse.

Similarly, expert members, despite their familiarity with specific subject matters, can benefit from training focused on parliamentary processes, effective communication strategies, and public engagement. Such training ensures that expert insights are not only rigorously scientific but also accessible and relevant to the broader societal context. Additionally, ongoing support for both lay and expert members, including access to research services and opportunities for skill development, can facilitate their continuous growth and effectiveness in their roles.

By addressing the foundational needs for authority, independence, and resources, and by empowering committee members with the knowledge and skills required to navigate the intricacies of policy scrutiny, Australia can enhance the capacity of its parliamentary committees. Through thoughtful implementation of these considerations, Australia can achieve a parliamentary committee system that is not only stronger and more effective but also more reflective of and responsive to the needs and aspirations of its citizens.

REFORM QUESTION TIME AS AN INTERROGATOR OF GOVERNMENTS

Reforming Question Time in the Australian federal parliament presents an opportunity to revitalise a key democratic institution. By learning from international practices and focusing on structural and rule-based reforms, it is possible to create a more informative, respectful, and effective session. These changes could lead to a more substantive debate, reduced partisan bickering, and increased public confidence in political processes.

WHY IS AUSTRALIA'S QUESTION TIME SO BAD?

The decline in the quality of debate during Question Time in the Australian Parliament is a multifaceted issue that has been years in the making, reflecting deep-seated problems within both the structural framework of the parliamentary system and the broader political culture. This deterioration has significant implications, not only for the functionality of Question Time as a mechanism for government accountability but also for public trust in political processes and institutions. The factors contributing to this decline encompass partisan politics, the format and rules of Question Time, media influence, cultural and behavioural norms, and structural limitations, each playing a part in undermining the session's effectiveness and public perception.

Partisan politics and the pursuit of point-scoring have significantly eroded the quality of debate during Question Time. The session often devolves into political theatre, with members more focused on scoring political points and achieving media coverage than on engaging in genuine inquiry or substantive debate. This approach, driven by a desire to undermine opponents rather than to interrogate policy matters constructively, results in a discourse that is more about opposition for its own sake than about the quality of governance or public interest.

The current format and rules governing Question Time further exacerbate these issues. Limited answer accountability allows ministers to deflect and avoid answering questions directly, diminishing the session's role as an accountability tool. Additionally, time constraints often prevent the in-depth exploration of complex issues, leading to oversimplification and responses that are more suited to soundbites than to detailed discussion.

Media influence also plays a critical role in shaping the conduct and public perception of Question Time. The media's focus on memorable one-liners and confrontational exchanges, driven by the quest for ratings and the evening news cycle, encourages participants to engage in behaviour that is more performative than substantive. This not only affects the nature of the debate itself but also shapes public perceptions of Question Time, often casting it in a light that emphasises drama and conflict over meaningful policy discussion.

Cultural and behavioural norms within Parliament have shifted over time, contributing to an erosion of decorum that is conducive to serious debate. Interruptions, heckling, and other disruptive behaviours have become more common, further detracting from the session's effectiveness. A diminishing respect for the institutional process of Question Time among some politicians has also led to its misuse as a platform for personal or party promotion, rather than for its intended purpose of government scrutiny.

Structural limitations within the parliamentary system also hinder the efficacy of Question Time. The dominance of the government in the parliamentary process, including Question Time, can stifle genuine scrutiny and reduce the incentive for meaningful dialogue. Additionally, the lack of an independent body to enforce rules and ensure the relevance and quality of questions and answers limits effective oversight and accountability during Question Time.

Addressing these challenges requires not only changes to the structure and rules of Question Time but also efforts to elevate the political discourse and re-evaluate the role of media in covering parliamentary proceedings. By tackling these issues head-on, there is potential to restore Question Time to its foundational purpose as a cornerstone of parliamentary democracy, enhancing government accountability, improving decision-making in the public interest, and ultimately rebuilding public trust in political institutions.

HISTORICAL CONTEXT AND PURPOSE

The institution of Question Time in Australian politics is deeply rooted in the traditions of parliamentary democracy, serving as a vital mechanism for transparency and accountability within the governmental framework. Its formal introduction in 1950 was guided by the principle that those in positions of power, particularly ministers, should be directly accountable to the legislature and, by extension, to the public they serve. This concept is foundational to the functioning of a democratic society, where elected officials are entrusted with significant responsibilities and must, therefore, be subject to rigorous scrutiny.

The original intent behind the establishment of Question Time was to provide a structured opportunity for ministers to be questioned about their decisions, policies, and the administration of their portfolios. This was aimed at ensuring that government actions remained aligned with legislative approval and public interest. By allowing members of the opposition, as well as those from the governing party, to pose questions, Question Time was designed to be a comprehensive accountability exercise. It embodied the democratic ideal that government should operate not in isolation but in constant dialogue with its legislature, reflecting a governance model that is both responsive and responsible.

However, the evolution of Question Time has seen it drift from its foundational purpose. What was conceived as a forum for substantive inquiry and accountability has, in many instances, transformed into a stage for political theatre. The session has increasingly been characterised by exchanges that prioritise political posturing and the scoring of rhetorical points over the pursuit of genuine accountability and transparency.

This shift has not only diluted the effectiveness of Question Time as a tool for democratic oversight but has also impacted public perception of the political process, with cynicism often overshadowing engagement.

Despite this drift, the historical significance and underlying purpose of Question Time remain undiminished. It represents a critical juncture in the parliamentary day, symbolising the direct line of accountability running from individual ministers to the Parliament and, by extension, to the Australian public. The ethos underpinning Question Time is that of ensuring that those who wield executive power are continually reminded of their duty to the electorate, providing explanations and justifications for their policy choices and administrative actions.

The challenge facing contemporary Australian politics is to reclaim the spirit of inquiry and accountability that originally motivated the establishment of Question Time. This involves not only a reflection on the procedural aspects that have allowed for its degeneration into political theatre but also a broader consideration of the cultural shifts needed within the political class to prioritise democratic accountability over partisan advantage.

INTERNATIONAL EXAMPLES OF EFFECTIVE USE

The practice of holding a designated time for questioning government officials is a feature present in several parliamentary democracies around the world. This practice is pivotal not only for the sake of transparency and accountability but also for enhancing public engagement with the political process. By examining the implementation and outcomes of these sessions in different countries, such as the United Kingdom's Prime Minister's Questions and the approach taken by Scandinavian parliaments, we can glean insights into their utility and effectiveness in fostering democratic values.

The United Kingdom's PMQs stand as one of the most renowned instances of this practice. PMQs offer a direct platform for Members of Parliament to question the Prime Minister on any aspect of national policy or current affairs. Despite facing criticisms over its confrontational tone and the spectacle it sometimes becomes, PMQs hold intrinsic value in promoting direct engagement between the government and its opposition. The very nature of live broadcast and the open format allows the public to witness firsthand the accountability mechanisms at work within their government. It not only serves as a tool for opposition and backbenchers to seek clarity and accountability from the Prime Minister but also acts as a significant driver of political engagement among the citizenry. The visibility of PMQs, coupled with the direct questioning format, helps demystify the operations of government, making political processes more accessible and understandable to the general public.

In contrast, some Scandinavian countries have adopted a more moderated and focused approach to their versions of Question Time. In these instances, questions must be submitted in advance, which affords government officials the opportunity to prepare more substantive and researched responses. This methodological difference aims to reduce the theatrics often associated with spontaneous questioning and seeks to enhance the quality and depth of discourse on policy matters.

The Scandinavian model emphasises the importance of constructive dialogue over confrontation, aiming to foster a more informative and less adversarial atmosphere. This approach aligns with the broader political culture in these countries, which often values consensus and comprehensive debate. By ensuring that questions are pre-submitted and responses well-researched, these parliaments facilitate a more detailed examination of issues, potentially leading to more informed public discourse and policy development.

The effectiveness and utility of Question Time or its equivalents in these and other parliamentary systems vary widely, influenced by the specific procedural rules in place, the political culture, and the degree to which these sessions are utilised as genuine tools for scrutiny versus opportunities for political posturing. In the best instances, these sessions serve to enhance transparency, hold government officials accountable, and engage the public in the legislative process. They offer a vital avenue for the airing of grievances, the clarification of policy positions, and the public demonstration of government accountability. However, the extent to which these objectives are achieved can depend significantly on the manner in which the sessions are conducted, the ethos of the political community, and the engagement of the public.

The differences in approach highlight the adaptability of this practice to different political cultures and systems, underscoring its potential to contribute positively to the democratic process. However, for these sessions to realise their full potential, they must be conducted with a genuine intent to scrutinise and inform, rather than just to grandstand or evade political scrutiny.

PROPOSED STRUCTURAL REFORMS

Reforming Question Time in Australian politics is not only a procedural necessity but a central step towards enhancing the democratic fabric of parliamentary governance. The current format of Question Time often falls short of its potential, and is mired in political theatrics and evasion. To redirect Question Time towards its foundational purpose of rigorous scrutiny and public interest, a series of structural reforms are proposed, aimed at fostering a more informative, respectful, and substantive discourse.

The introduction of advance notice for questions represents a significant shift from the spontaneity that characterises the current practice. While potentially reducing the element of surprise, requiring questions to be submitted in advance can lead to more thoughtful, researched, and comprehensive answers. This approach minimises the opportunity for ministers to deflect questions with prepared, generic responses, instead obliging them to engage with the specifics of the inquiry. Such a reform could significantly enhance the informative value of Question Time, making it a more genuine exercise in scrutiny and accountability.

An independent moderation of Question Time could serve as a cornerstone for elevating the quality of discourse and decorum within the session. By entrusting an impartial figure—as is the case with independent speaker in the British Parliament, who must sever all ties with their political party while in office—or a body with the oversight of proceedings, the parliamentary exchange is more likely to remain focused, direct, and free from the partisan bickering that often detracts from its substantive potential. Independent moderation could ensure that questions are addressed with the seriousness they deserve and that deviations from the topic at hand are curtailed.

Adjusting the time allocation and format of Question Time is crucial for allowing a deeper exploration of issues. Extending the duration of both questions and answers, coupled with a format that permits immediate follow-up questions, can encourage a more thorough investigation into policy matters. This adjustment would facilitate a dialogue that moves beyond surface-level engagement, enabling a genuine debate that can illuminate complex aspects of governance and policy.

The implementation of strict relevance rules is essential for maintaining the integrity of Question Time. By requiring that responses be directly relevant to the questions posed, evasion and obfuscation can be significantly reduced. Such rules would compel ministers to address the substance of inquiries, ensuring that Question Time fulfills its role as a mechanism for accountability.

To reinforce these structural changes, clear penalties for non-compliance are necessary. Establishing and enforcing consequences for those who flout the rules of Question Time serves as a deterrent against the reduction of parliamentary exchanges to political point-scoring. This measure would underscore the seriousness with which parliamentary scrutiny is regarded and promote a more disciplined approach to engagement.

Encouraging policy-focused questions is another vital reform. By fostering a culture that prioritises the understanding and examination of policy decisions over the pursuit of political advantage, Question Time can become a forum for meaningful discourse on national issues. This shift would not only enhance the quality of parliamentary debate but also elevate the public's perception of political engagement.

These proposed reforms offer a roadmap for revitalising Question Time in Australia. By instituting measures that enhance the informative quality, relevance, and decorum of the session, Question Time can be transformed into a more effective instrument of parliamentary scrutiny, one that serves the public interest with rigour and integrity.

RESTORING PUBLIC CONFIDENCE IN POLITICS

Reforming Question Time in the Australian Parliament holds the potential to significantly elevate public trust in government, enhance accountability, and promote decision-making that aligns more closely with the public interest. At the heart of this potential transformation is a dual approach that emphasises both the procedural aspects of Question Time and the broader engagement with and education of the public about its role and significance. By making Question Time more transparent, accessible, and comprehensible, and by actively engaging the public in understanding its function, the Australian Parliament can bridge the gap that often exists between the electorate and their elected representatives. Transparency and accessibility are foundational to this reformative effort. By enhancing the broadcasting of Question Time and incorporating explanatory commentary that elucidates the proceedings, the Parliament can demystify what often appears to the public as a convoluted or opaque process. Such efforts could involve the use of modern digital platforms to stream sessions, accompanied by real-time analysis or summaries that break down complex parliamentary jargon into understandable language. This approach not only makes Question Time more accessible to a wider audience but also invites the public into the heart of democratic processes, allowing them to witness firsthand the mechanisms of accountability at work. By providing clear, accessible insights into the questioning and answer sessions, the Parliament can foster a more informed public discourse, contributing to a more engaged and politically literate electorate.

The nexus between reforming Question Time and improving public trust in government is clear. As the process becomes more transparent, accessible, and understood, the public's confidence in political institutions is likely to increase. This heightened trust stems from a greater visibility of accountability mechanisms and an enhanced understanding of how elected officials are held to account for their decisions and policies.

When the electorate sees that their concerns and the broader issues facing society are being directly addressed in Parliament, their faith in the democratic process and in those who govern on their behalf is strengthened.

Improved accountability through reformed Question Time can also lead to better decision-making in the public interest. As ministers are compelled to provide thorough and meaningful responses to questions, the quality of public discourse around policy and governance is enriched. This, in turn, can inform more nuanced and well-considered policy decisions, reflecting a deeper engagement with the issues and challenges at hand.

Reforming Question Time in the Australian Parliament has the potential to profoundly impact the relationship between the government and the governed. This transformation not only benefits the immediate political landscape but also strengthens the democratic fabric of Australian society, promoting a more informed, engaged, and empowered electorate.

*

CHAPTER 5: MEDIA AND INFORMATION

Improving public broadcasting in Australia centres on bolstering the independence, diversity, and quality of public media outlets like the ABC. This can be achieved through enhanced financial support, legislative protections against political and commercial pressures, and commitments to content diversity that mirrors the diversity of Australian society. Embracing digital transformation and innovating in content delivery are crucial to staying relevant in the rapidly evolving media landscape. Strengthening governance and fostering collaborations can further ensure public broadcasters serve the broad spectrum of Australian interests and cultures effectively. By implementing these strategies, Australia can fortify its public broadcasting sector, making it a robust, independent, and diverse pillar of the media ecosystem.

REINFORCE FINANCIAL SUPPORT FOR PUBLIC MEDIA

In recent years, the Australian Broadcasting Corporation has faced a series of financial constraints and budget cuts—at least $783 million during the term of the Coalition government between 2013 and 2022—that have sparked significant concern among advocates of public broadcasting and media diversity. These cuts are often perceived as part of broader conservative attacks on the institution, aiming to undermine its ability to operate independently and effectively fulfill its mandate. This situation has led to calls for a reinforcement of financial support for the ABC, recognising its crucial role in the Australian media landscape.

The ABC, as a public broadcaster, occupies a unique and invaluable position in Australia's democracy. It serves not only as a source of news and information but also as a platform for diverse voices and stories that reflect the rich tapestry of Australian society. However, the ability of the ABC to continue fulfilling these roles has been jeopardised by financial challenge and commitment to the public interest that has almost been discarded by successive conservative appointments to the ABC Board of Management. Reduced funding has implications for the breadth and quality of content that can be produced, potentially diminishing the broadcaster's capacity to invest in comprehensive news coverage, innovative programming, and digital media initiatives.

Reinforcing financial support for the ABC would counteract these negative impacts, enabling the broadcaster to maintain and expand its services. Increased funding—or at least, more effective financial management—is essential to ensure that the ABC can continue to produce high-quality, diverse content that meets the needs and interests of all Australians. This includes investing in investigative journalism, which plays a vital role in holding power to account, and in children's programming that educates and entertains the next generation. Stable financial support would allow the ABC to embrace technological advancements and innovate in the digital space, ensuring it remains relevant in a rapidly evolving media landscape.

Beyond the practical aspects of funding, reinforcing financial support for the ABC sends a strong message about the value placed on public broadcasting in Australia. It reflects a commitment to media diversity, editorial independence, and the principle that access to high-quality, factual information is a public good and in the interests of the community. In an era characterised by misinformation and media concentration, the ABC's role as a trusted and impartial news source is more important than ever.

This call for increased financial support is not just about countering past budget cuts. It's about looking forward and ensuring that the ABC has the resources to innovate and adapt to future challenges. Whether it's enhancing its digital platforms, expanding its international coverage, or developing new ways to engage with audiences, the ABC must have the financial stability to pursue these objectives without compromising its core mission. While the Labor government did announce additional funding of $83.7 million in 2022 and introduced a five-year funding cycle to enhance funding certainty, at present, this is still a function that can be undone by future governments which have no interest in public broadcasting, and it needs to be protected.

By committing to the financial sustainability of the ABC, Australia can ensure that this vital institution remains strong, vibrant, and capable of meeting the challenges of the twenty-first century. This is not just an investment in a broadcaster but an investment in the cultural and democratic fabric of the nation itself.

LEGISLATIVE PROTECTIONS FOR THE ABC

In the evolving landscape of media and communication, the ABC should stand as a beacon of impartiality and integrity, serving the public interest free from the sway of political and commercial pressures. Yet, this ideal state is continually threatened by conservative governments that are intent on destroying the ABC, and the inherent nature of the current media environment, where political and commercial interests often seek to leverage media platforms for their own ends. It is within this context that the call for robust legislative protections for public broadcasters emerges as a critical discourse, aiming to safeguard their operational independence and ensure their ability to serve the public good without undue influence.

The essence of legislative protections for entities like the ABC is to enshrine in law the principles that guarantee freedom from interference, ensuring that these institutions can carry out their mandates to inform, educate, and entertain in a manner that is both impartial and diverse. Such protections are not just administrative formalities but foundational to the preservation of a democratic society, where access to unbiased information is paramount. These laws must be designed to withstand the ebbs and flows of political change, ensuring that no government or commercial entity can easily undermine the broadcaster's independence.

The need for these protections stems from a recognition of the subtle and not-so-subtle ways in which interference can manifest. From the allocation of funding to the appointment of board members, opportunities abound for external pressures to influence editorial decisions and organisational priorities. Legislative measures must address these vulnerabilities directly, establishing clear and unassailable guidelines for funding, governance, and operational autonomy. Similarly, the process for appointing board members and senior executives should be insulated from political influence, through the involvement of independent panels or bipartisan committees.

These legislative frameworks must also include provisions that ensure transparency and accountability without compromising editorial freedom. While public broadcasters must be accountable to the public they serve, this accountability should not provide a backdoor for political interference. Instead, it should foster a culture of openness, encouraging public broadcasters to engage with their audiences in meaningful ways, to listen to their concerns, and to reflect on their feedback, all while maintaining editorial independence.

The implementation or reinforcement of legislative protections for public broadcasters also signals a broader commitment to the principles of democracy and pluralism. It acknowledges the role of public media as a space for diverse voices and perspectives, serving as a counterbalance to the concentration of media ownership and the proliferation of misinformation. In safeguarding the independence of the ABC and similar institutions, legislation acts as a bulwark against the forces that threaten to diminish the quality and diversity of public discourse.

In crafting these protections, it is essential to strike a balance between independence and accountability, ensuring that public broadcasters are neither beholden to the whims of political and commercial interests nor operating in a vacuum without regard to the public interest. This balance is delicate and requires ongoing vigilance to maintain, but it is essential for preserving the trust and confidence of the public in their national broadcasters.

CONTENT DIVERSITY AND QUALITY

The ABC has long held the responsibility—and, quite often, unfulfilled—of mirroring the rich and diverse fabric of Australian society through its content. However, criticisms have been raised about the lack of diversity and quality in public broadcasting, with particular concern for the representation of Indigenous Australians and other underrepresented communities.

These concerns spotlight the urgent need for a concerted effort to promote content diversity and quality, ensuring that the narratives shared and voices heard reflect the true heterogeneity of the Australian populace.

Promoting content diversity and quality in public broadcasting is not just an issue of fulfilling quotas or ticking boxes; it's about enriching the national conversation, fostering a deeper understanding among different communities, and promoting a sense of belonging and identity. It acknowledges that Australian society is a mosaic of cultures, perspectives, and experiences, and that each piece of this mosaic has value and should be represented in the media landscape.

To achieve this, public broadcasters must be encouraged or mandated to produce content that spans the breadth of Australia's cultural, linguistic, and regional diversity. This entails not just the inclusion of diverse faces on screen but also the diversification of voices behind the scenes—writers, directors, producers, and other key roles—ensuring that the content is authentically representative of the varied experiences within Australian society. Such a strategy must include a committed effort to elevate Indigenous stories and voices, acknowledging their unique place in the nation's history and cultural landscape.

The commitment to diversity must also extend to the types of content produced. This encompasses a wide range of genres—from news and current affairs to drama, children's programming, and documentaries. Each offers a different avenue for storytelling and engagement, appealing to various segments of the audience and providing multiple platforms for diverse voices to be heard.

However, promoting diversity in content is not enough on its own; the quality of this content is equally important. Quality, in this context, means content that is well-researched, creatively produced, and which resonates with authenticity and relevance. It means investing in the skills and talents of creators from diverse backgrounds, providing them with the resources and platforms to tell their stories compellingly and professionally. Quality content is what engages audiences, prompts reflection, and fosters understanding and empathy among different segments of society.

Addressing the challenge of content diversity and quality also requires a responsive and dynamic approach to content development and distribution. In an age where digital platforms are increasingly becoming the primary means of content consumption, public broadcasters need to leverage these technologies to reach wider and more diverse audiences. This includes not only the traditional broadcasting mediums but also online platforms, social media, and mobile applications, each offering unique opportunities for engagement and storytelling. Promoting content diversity and quality in public broadcasting necessitates ongoing dialogue with communities across Australia. This dialogue should aim to understand their needs, aspirations, and concerns, ensuring that the content not only represents them but also serves them. It means listening to feedback, being open to criticism, and being willing to evolve and adapt in response to changing societal dynamics.

The push for greater content diversity and quality in public broadcasting is a call to deepen the national discourse, to enrich Australian media with the threads of all its communities. It is an acknowledgment that every Australian, regardless of their background, has a story worth telling and a voice worth hearing. By committing to this goal, public broadcasters can play a crucial role in fostering a more inclusive, empathetic, and united society, reflecting the true spirit of Australia in all its diversity.

INNOVATION AND DIGITAL EXPANSION IN PUBLIC BROADCASTING

In the rapidly evolving digital era, the transformation of media consumption patterns poses both a challenge and an opportunity for public broadcasters. Traditional platforms such as free-to-air television, print media, and radio are witnessing a decline in their audience base, as consumers, especially the younger demographics, increasingly turn to digital platforms for content consumption. This shift necessitates a strategic shift towards innovation and digital expansion, enabling public broadcasters to remain relevant, accessible, and engaging in the digital age.

The imperative for innovation and digital expansion is not only about transitioning existing content onto digital platforms but reimagining public broadcasting in the context of the digital landscape. This involves investing in digital infrastructure that supports the seamless delivery of content across various digital platforms, including online streaming services, mobile applications, and social media. Such investment ensures that public broadcasters can provide high-quality, interactive, and on-demand content, meeting the expectations of a digitally savvy audience.

Innovation within public broadcasting must go beyond infrastructure and embrace content creation and distribution strategies that resonate with the digital-first audience. This includes leveraging data analytics and artificial intelligence to understand audience preferences and behaviours—without simply relying on 'click-bait' methods of engagement—enabling the creation of personalised and engaging content. It also involves exploring content formats such as podcasts, web series, and interactive storytelling, which have gained significant traction among younger audiences. While the ABC is currently engaged in some of these areas, it needs to do more to engage with local community producers to create more diverse content.

Digital expansion also offers an opportunity for public broadcasters to enhance their social media engagement. Social media platforms are not just channels for content distribution but spaces for building communities and fostering interactive relationships with audiences. By effectively leveraging these platforms, public broadcasters can increase their reach, engage in real-time conversations with their audience, and become more responsive to the public discourse. This requires a strategic approach to social media, one that prioritises engagement, interaction and narrowcasting, over broadcasting.

The push towards digital innovation within public broadcasting underscores the need for digital literacy and accessibility. As public broadcasters expand their digital footprint, it is imperative to ensure that their content is accessible to all segments of the population, including those with limited digital skills or access. This involves creating user-friendly platforms, providing digital literacy programs, and ensuring that content is accessible to people with disabilities.

The journey towards innovation and digital expansion also necessitates a cultural shift within public broadcasting organisations.

This shift involves embracing a culture of innovation, where experimentation and risk-taking are encouraged, and where there is a continuous quest for improvement and adaptation. It requires building capabilities in digital technologies and fostering a workforce that is agile, digitally proficient, and aligned with the vision of a modern public broadcaster.

The digital transformation of the media landscape and shift away from free-to-air broadcasting presents a critical moment for public broadcasters, not just in Australia, but internationally. By embracing innovation and expanding their digital presence, public broadcasters like the ABC can navigate the challenges of declining traditional platforms and meet the evolving needs of their audience. This not only ensures their continued relevance and sustainability but also enhances their ability to fulfill their public service mandate in the digital age. Through strategic investment in digital infrastructure, content innovation, and audience engagement, public broadcasters can continue to serve as trusted, inclusive, and dynamic sources of information, entertainment, and education for all Australians.

STRENGTHEN GOVERNANCE AND ACCOUNTABILITY

Over the years, the ABC has encountered challenges that have brought into sharp focus the need for robust governance structures capable of withstanding political pressures and interference. The experiences under the administrations spanning from Howard government between 1996 to 2007, and the Abbott–Turnbull–Morrison governments between 2013 to 2022, have underscored the vulnerability of public broadcasting to the whims of political agendas, making the call for strengthened governance and accountability both timely and critical.

At the heart of this issue is the imperative to ensure that the governance structures of the ABC not only profess but practice independence from political influence, safeguarding the broadcaster's ability to serve the public interest. This entails a thorough revision and fortification of the processes by which board members and executives are appointed, emphasising transparency, merit, and independence. The objective is to cultivate a governance body that reflects a broad spectrum of expertise and perspectives, free from the shackles of political partisanship, and committed to upholding the principles of public broadcasting.

Strengthening governance also involves enhancing the accountability mechanisms to which the ABC is subject. Accountability, in this context, extends beyond financial audits and performance reviews; it encompasses the broadcaster's adherence to its charter, its commitment to impartiality, and its responsiveness to the needs and concerns of the Australian public. This requires the establishment of clear, objective criteria for evaluating the broadcaster's performance, alongside accessible channels through which the public can voice feedback, criticisms, and commendations.

The issue of political interference in public broadcasting is not unique to Australia; it is a challenge faced by public broadcasters around the world.

Australia has the opportunity to lead by example, implementing governance and accountability frameworks that could serve as a benchmark for public media worldwide. This involves a commitment to continuous review and adaptation of these frameworks, ensuring they remain relevant and effective in the face of evolving political, technological, and societal landscapes.

Strengthening governance and accountability at the ABC necessitates an engaged and informed public. The Australian people must be active participants in the discourse surrounding public broadcasting, advocating for policies that ensure its independence and holding it to account. Public support for the ABC, and demand for its independence, is a powerful counterbalance to political pressures, reinforcing the broadcaster's mandate to serve the public interest above all.

PARTNERSHIPS AND COLLABORATIONS FOR THE FUTURE

The landscape of public broadcasting is not only shaped by the content it produces but also by the relationships it fosters with other entities in the pursuit of serving the public interest. For the ABC, forming partnerships and collaborations with a variety of organisations opens avenues to enrich its content offerings, promote cultural exchange, and ultimately serve its audience more effectively. In an era where the dissemination of information and cultural literacy are paramount, such collaborations stand as pillars supporting the broad mission of public broadcasting.

Partnerships with educational institutions stand out as a particularly fruitful avenue for the ABC. While the ABC currently has the TOP 5 arrangement with University of Sydney, University of Melbourne and Australian National University, and Creative Australia, this is a field that could be explored and enhanced further.

By collaborating with universities, schools, and vocational training centres, the ABC can develop educational content that is not only informative but also aligned with curricular goals and learning outcomes. Such collaborations could lead to the production of specialised programming for children and adults alike, ranging from science and technology to arts and humanities. This synergy between broadcasters and educators could significantly enhance the educational landscape, making learning more accessible and engaging through multimedia resources.

Cultural organisations, including museums, art galleries, and music ensembles, offer another rich vein of potential partnerships. Collaborations in this domain could facilitate the creation of content that showcases Australia's cultural heritage and contemporary artistic expressions, promoting cultural literacy and appreciation among the public.

These partnerships could take various forms, from broadcasting live cultural events to developing documentary series that delve into Australia's artistic and cultural history. By bringing the arts into homes across the country, the ABC can play a pivotal role in fostering a sense of national identity and pride.

International broadcasting services present a unique opportunity for the ABC to promote cultural exchange and broaden its audience's perspective on global issues. Partnerships with international broadcasters could lead to the exchange of content, co-production of programs, and sharing of best practices. Such initiatives not only enrich the ABC's content library with diverse perspectives but also position the broadcaster as a global player in the public media space. Through these international collaborations, the ABC can offer its audience a window to the world, facilitating a better understanding of global cultures, issues, and events.

The digital realm offers additional possibilities for partnerships, particularly with technology companies and digital platforms. Collaborations in this area could enhance the ABC's digital capabilities, from improving content delivery systems to developing new interactive media experiences. Such partnerships could also provide the ABC with access to cutting-edge technologies and expertise, enabling the broadcaster to innovate and stay ahead in the rapidly evolving media landscape.

Collaborations with non-profit organisations and community groups could also help the ABC to reach and serve underserved communities more effectively. By working together, they can identify the unique needs and interests of diverse groups within Australia, developing content and initiatives that address these areas. This approach not only ensures that the ABC's content is inclusive and representative but also strengthens the broadcaster's role as a unifying force within the community.

WORK TOWARDS TRUTH IN JOURNALISM

Addressing the challenges of misinformation and ensuring truth in journalism in Australia requires a multi-faceted approach. Strengthening the regulatory capabilities of the Australian Press Council is paramount to overseeing ethical standards in journalism. Educating the public on media literacy and supporting independent fact-checking services are essential steps to empower individuals to critically engage with news content. Legal frameworks must hold media entities accountable for spreading falsehoods, while policies should promote a diverse and pluralistic media environment. Collaborations across sectors can drive innovation in detecting and countering misinformation, and a greater emphasis on investigative journalism will ensure in-depth and accurate reporting. Together, these strategies can help safeguard the integrity of journalism and ensure the Australian public has access to reliable and truthful information.

STRENGTHENING THE AUSTRALIAN PRESS COUNCIL

The Australian Press Council should be an important institution in the landscape of Australian media, which is tasked with the critical role of upholding journalistic standards and serving as a watchdog for ethical journalism. It doesn't do its job. The efficacy and impartiality of the Press Council have come under scrutiny, with criticisms highlighting its perceived limitations in autonomy, resources, and authority.

Funded by commercial media interests, the Press Council is often seen as a "toothless tiger," more aligned with the interests of the media industry than those of the public it is meant to serve. In light of these challenges, there is a pressing need to re-envision and strengthen the Press Council, transforming it into a robust body capable of effectively overseeing and regulating news media practices, enforcing ethical standards, and adjudicating complaints with efficiency and fairness. The poor state of Australian mainstream journalism and media reporting can be directly attributable to the ineffectiveness of the National Press Council.

The foundation of a strengthened Press Council lies in enhancing its independence. Currently, its funding model, primarily reliant on contributions from commercial media entities, poses a significant conflict of interest, compromising the council's ability to act decisively against these very entities. To mitigate this, exploring alternative funding mechanisms is important. Government funding, though a possible solution, carries its own risks of political interference. A more viable approach could involve a mixed funding model that combines government funds with contributions from a wider array of stakeholders, including public donations and grants from independent foundations. This model should be designed to safeguard the Press Council's operational independence, ensuring that no single source of funding can exert undue influence.

Enhancing the powers and resources of the Press Council is another critical step. This entails not only increasing its financial and human resources but also expanding its legal and regulatory authority to enforce compliance and impose sanctions on media outlets that violate ethical standards. The current self-regulatory framework relies heavily on the goodwill of media organisations to adhere to the Press Council's rulings, which can be ineffective in compelling change. Granting the Press Council statutory powers, similar to those held by regulatory bodies in other sectors, could significantly amplify its ability to enforce standards and ensure accountability within the industry.

Improving the efficiency and transparency of the complaint handling process is also essential. For many, the process appears opaque and cumbersome, discouraging public engagement and undermining trust in the council's role as a mediator between the media and the public. Streamlining complaint procedures, ensuring timely responses, and making the process more user-friendly can enhance public confidence in the Press Council' ability to address grievances. Additionally, increasing transparency about the outcomes of complaints and the rationale behind decisions can further reinforce this trust.

A strengthened Press Council should also proactively work to elevate media standards across the industry. This involves not only reacting to breaches of ethical conduct but also setting positive standards for quality journalism. Through initiatives like training programs for journalists, research on media ethics, and public education campaigns about media literacy, the Press Council could play a transformative role in fostering a culture of integrity and excellence in journalism. These efforts can help to build a more informed and critical audience, which in turn can exert pressure on media outlets to uphold high standards.

Fostering a closer collaboration with other stakeholders in the media ecosystem, including digital platforms, educational institutions, and civil society organisations, can amplify the impact of the Press Council. The challenges facing journalism today, from the spread of misinformation to the financial pressures on quality reporting, require a coordinated response. By working in partnership with these stakeholders, the Press Council can contribute to a more resilient and ethical media landscape. Such an environment is crucial for the health of Australian democracy, ensuring that the public has access to reliable and high-quality information.

PROMOTING MEDIA LITERACY

In an era characterised by an unprecedented deluge of information, the ability to navigate the media landscape with discernment and critical thinking is more crucial than ever. Australia, despite boasting one of the most robust education systems globally, finds its populace increasingly besieged by misinformation and political scare campaigns, highlighting a glaring need for a concerted effort to enhance media literacy across the nation. Promoting media literacy is not only an educational initiative but a fundamental societal imperative, aimed at empowering Australians to critically evaluate news sources, recognise media bias, and distinguish between misinformation, disinformation and factual reporting.

While this would be a long-term solution, the crux of improving media literacy in Australia hinges on integrating comprehensive media literacy programs into the national educational curriculum. Such programs should be designed to cultivate critical thinking, analytical skills, and a nuanced understanding of the media's role in society from an early age. By embedding media literacy into the fabric of education, from primary through to tertiary levels, students can develop the capacity to question and critique the information they encounter, fostering a generation of informed, discerning citizens capable of navigating the complexities of the modern information ecosystem.

The pursuit of media literacy extends beyond formal education settings, necessitating broad-based initiatives that engage the wider community. Public awareness campaigns, workshops, and lifelong learning programs can play central roles in reaching adults and seniors, demographics that are often overlooked in digital literacy efforts but are equally susceptible to misinformation. Such initiatives can be spearheaded by a coalition of stakeholders, including government agencies, non-profit organisations, media outlets, and academic institutions, each contributing their expertise and resources to cultivate a media-savvy public.

Central to the endeavour of promoting media literacy is the need to address the evolving nature of the media landscape itself, particularly the rise of digital and social media platforms. The proliferation of these platforms has democratised information dissemination, but it has also facilitated the spread of misinformation and echo chambers. Educational programs and public initiatives must, therefore, equip individuals with the skills to critically assess digital content, understand algorithms' role in shaping their information exposure, and engage constructively in online discourse.

Another critical element in enhancing media literacy is fostering a culture of skepticism and inquiry. Encouraging individuals to question the veracity of information, check multiple sources, and seek out reputable news outlets can mitigate the impact of misinformation. This requires not only teaching technical skills, such as how to fact-check information, but also cultivating an attitude of critical engagement with media content.

Promoting media literacy in Australia must be an inclusive effort that recognises the diverse needs and vulnerabilities of different community groups. Tailored programs that consider linguistic, cultural, and socioeconomic factors can ensure that media literacy initiatives are accessible and relevant to all Australians, including Indigenous communities, non-English speaking backgrounds, and rural populations.

ENCOURAGING FACT-CHECKING SERVICES

The proliferation of misinformation and the rapid pace at which it spreads across digital platforms pose significant challenges to societies worldwide, undermining public trust in media and democratic institutions. In Australia, where the media landscape is not immune to these global trends, the establishment and support of independent fact-checking services emerge as a crucial strategy for safeguarding the integrity of the public discourse. Encouraging such services requires a nuanced approach that balances the need for rigorous fact-checking with concerns over government overreach and the financial sustainability of media operations.

The first step towards fostering a robust fact-checking ecosystem is the recognition of its importance not just by the government, but also by media organisations, non-profit entities, and the public. Independent fact-checking services serve as a critical line of defence against misinformation, providing real-time analyses of news content to verify its accuracy. However, their effectiveness hinges on their independence and the trust they engender among the public and within the media industry.

One viable model for supporting these services without precipitating government overreach is the establishment of a multi-stakeholder fund. Such a fund could draw on contributions from the government, private sector, philanthropic organisations, and potentially a nominal fee from media outlets themselves. This diversified funding model would mitigate the risk of undue influence by any single entity, preserving the independence of the fact-checking services. It would also address the financial constraints faced by the media sector, distributing the cost of fact-checking across a broader base of stakeholders who have a vested interest in the integrity of public discourse.

Another model involves leveraging partnerships between academic institutions and the media. Universities and research institutions possess the expertise, resources, and credibility to conduct in-depth fact-checking and analysis. By forming partnerships with media outlets, these institutions can provide fact-checking services that not only enhance the accuracy of news reporting but also offer educational opportunities for journalism students. Such collaborations can be financially sustainable, benefiting from the existing infrastructure and resources of academic institutions while providing real-world learning experiences for the next generation of journalists.

Media outlets could also be encouraged to adopt internal fact-checking mechanisms as part of their editorial processes. While this approach requires investment, the long-term benefits of increased credibility and audience trust can outweigh the initial costs. Media organisations can also explore innovative technological solutions, such as artificial intelligence and machine learning algorithms, to assist in identifying potentially false or misleading information.

These technologies can streamline the fact-checking process, making it more efficient and cost-effective.

Encouraging the development and visibility of independent fact-checking services in Australia necessitates a collaborative, multi-faceted strategy that addresses the dual challenges of ensuring independence and financial sustainability. By combining diversified funding models, partnerships with academic institutions, internal fact-checking mechanisms within media outlets, and public education efforts, Australia can build a robust fact-checking ecosystem. This ecosystem would not only counteract the spread of misinformation but also reinforce the foundations of a well-informed democratic society, enhancing the credibility and trustworthiness of the media landscape.

LEGISLATIVE AND POLICY MEASURES

In the contemporary media environment, characterised by the rapid dissemination of information and the pervasive influence of digital platforms, the challenge of countering misinformation and disinformation has become a pressing concern. In Australia, as in many democracies worldwide, the integrity of the public discourse is foundational to the health of the democratic process. Recognising the detrimental effects of misinformation on society, there is a growing consensus on the need for legislative and policy measures to hold media companies accountable for the content they disseminate. Crafting such measures requires a delicate balance between safeguarding freedom of expression—a cornerstone of democratic societies—and preventing the spread of harmful misinformation.

A crucial first step in addressing this challenge is the clear definition of *misinformation* and *disinformation* within the legal framework. Misinformation refers to false or inaccurate information spread without malicious intent, whereas disinformation is deliberately designed to deceive and mislead. Establishing legal definitions for these terms is essential for identifying and categorising content that may harm the public interest. This distinction also helps to safeguard against the infringement of free speech, ensuring that measures target maliciously false content without encroaching on the expression of genuine opinions and analyses.

One legislative approach to hold media companies accountable involves the introduction of laws that mandate transparency in content sourcing and labeling. Media companies could be required to disclose the origins of the information they publish and to label content that has been fact-checked or disputed by credible sources. This policy not only aids consumers in navigating the information landscape but also encourages media outlets to exercise due diligence in verifying the content they disseminate.

The establishment of a regulatory body dedicated to monitoring and addressing misinformation could be instrumental in enforcing these standards. This entity would operate independently of government and media organisations, equipped with the authority to investigate complaints, assess content for misinformation, and apply sanctions as necessary. Sanctions could range from fines for media companies that repeatedly spread harmful misinformation to mandatory retractions and corrections for specific instances of disinformation. Such a body would also serve as a mediator between the public and media organisations, providing a structured avenue for addressing concerns related to misinformation.

Incentives for adherence to best practices in journalism represent another policy measure that could complement legislative actions. These incentives might include tax breaks, grants, or other financial benefits for media companies that implement rigorous fact-checking procedures and adhere to ethical standards in reporting. Conversely, media outlets that fail to meet these standards could face penalties, such as increased scrutiny from regulatory bodies or exclusion from participating in publicly funded advertising campaigns.

In addition, collaboration with digital platforms is crucial in the fight against misinformation. Legislative measures could require platforms to implement more robust content moderation policies, promote authoritative information sources, and demote or remove proven misinformation. While this approach raises concerns about censorship and the role of tech companies in policing content, transparent guidelines and independent oversight can help mitigate these risks, ensuring that actions taken against misinformation are justified and balanced.

By carefully balancing the imperative to counter misinformation with the need to uphold freedom of expression, Australia can establish a regulatory framework that promotes a well-informed, resilient society. Through clear legal definitions, transparency requirements, independent oversight, incentives for ethical journalism, and collaboration with digital platforms, Australia can pave the way for a media environment that fosters trust, accountability, and democratic engagement.

FOSTERING DIVERSE MEDIA VOICES

The landscape of Australian media, with its limited diversity and high concentration of media ownership, reflects broader global challenges within the industry. In Australia, the dominance of major players like News Corporation has raised concerns about the plurality of voices and perspectives available in the public sphere. The situation is compounded by the homogeneity within the journalistic ranks, where individuals from predominantly Anglo, white, and exclusive private school backgrounds are overrepresented. This lack of diversity in media voices not only narrows the range of discourse but also fails to reflect the multicultural and diverse fabric of Australian society. Addressing this issue is not just about enriching the media landscape; it's about strengthening democracy itself by ensuring that all segments of society have their views represented and their stories told.

Encouraging the growth of independent and diverse media outlets is a critical step towards achieving a more pluralistic media environment. This endeavour requires a multi-faceted approach, combining financial support, policy initiatives, and educational efforts. Grants, subsidies, and support programs targeted at emerging media outlets can provide the financial lifeline needed for these organisations to establish themselves and thrive. Such financial assistance should be designed to lower the barriers to entry for underrepresented voices, including those from Indigenous communities, migrant backgrounds, and other minority groups. By providing seed funding, operational grants, and subsidies for training and development, the government and philanthropic organisations can play a pivotal role in nurturing a diverse media ecosystem.

However, financial support alone is not sufficient. Policy measures that encourage diversity and counteract monopolisation are equally important. Implementing regulations that limit the concentration of media ownership and promote competition can help ensure that no single entity has disproportionate influence over the public discourse. In addition, policies that require broadcasters and publishers to demonstrate commitment to diversity as a condition of licensing could provide an incentive to existing media companies to broaden their recruitment and content strategies.

The call for a Royal Commission into Media Diversity by the Australian Greens highlights the need for a comprehensive examination of the state of media plurality in Australia. Such an inquiry could provide a detailed assessment of the challenges and barriers to diversity within the media industry and offer recommendations for reform. While the Labor government's reluctance to initiate such a commission may stem from various political considerations, the establishment of an independent body to investigate these issues remains a crucial step toward informed and effective action.

Fostering diverse media voices extends beyond the realm of traditional news media. The rise of digital platforms and social media has democratised content creation, offering new avenues for diverse voices to be heard. Supporting digital literacy and content creation skills among underrepresented groups can empower these communities to tell their own stories and engage with a wider audience. This includes providing training programs, access to technology, and platforms that amplify marginalised voices.

Educational initiatives aimed at diversifying the pipeline of future media professionals are also vital. Scholarships, internships, and mentorship programs targeting students from diverse backgrounds can help break down the barriers to entry into the media profession. Collaborations between media organisations, educational institutions, and community groups can nurture talent and provide pathways for diverse individuals to enter and succeed in the media industry.

PARTNERSHIPS FOR TRUTHFUL REPORTING

The contemporary media landscape is fraught with challenges, among which the proliferation of misinformation stands as a formidable adversary to public trust and informed discourse. In Australia, as in many parts of the world, there is a pressing need for innovative solutions to enhance the accuracy and integrity of news reporting. One promising approach is the establishment of partnerships for truthful reporting between media organisations, academic institutions, and technology companies. These collaborations aim to harness collective expertise and resources to develop new technologies and methodologies that can bolster the fight against misinformation.

The synergy between media organisations, academic institutions, and technology companies creates a fertile ground for addressing the complex issue of misinformation. Media organisations bring to the table their expertise in journalism and content creation, along with a deep understanding of the challenges inherent in maintaining editorial integrity in the digital age. Academic institutions contribute research capabilities and theoretical insights into media studies, psychology, and information technology. Technology companies offer the technical prowess needed to develop and implement solutions at scale, from sophisticated algorithms that detect fake news to platforms that facilitate the verification of sources.

Looking beyond Australia, several countries have made strides in fostering partnerships for truthful reporting, each providing valuable lessons on the efficacy of such collaborations.

Canada: The Canadian Journalism Foundation, in partnership with leading academic and media entities, has launched initiatives aimed at enhancing media literacy and promoting fact-checking practices. These efforts aim not only to equip journalists with the tools to combat misinformation but also to educate the public on discerning credible information. The collaborative nature of these initiatives underscores the importance of a multifaceted approach to truthful reporting.

New Zealand: New Zealand's approach to truthful reporting has emphasised the role of public broadcasting, with Radio New Zealand partnering with local universities to investigate misinformation trends and develop educational content. This partnership leverages RNZ's reach and the academic community's research capabilities to foster a more informed and critical audience.

Western Europe: Several countries in Western Europe have seen successful collaborations between media organisations and technology firms to implement advanced fact-checking tools and algorithms. For instance, the BBC's Reality Check team works alongside tech companies and academic experts to develop innovative approaches to verify content and educate the public. These efforts have contributed to a media environment that is increasingly vigilant against misinformation.

The international examples highlight a common outcome: partnerships for truthful reporting can lead to better reporting cultures that prioritise accuracy and integrity. Such collaborations have the potential to create a virtuous cycle where trustworthy reporting gains public confidence, which in turn demands higher standards of truthfulness from all media outlets. Furthermore, these partnerships can accelerate the adoption of innovative technologies and methodologies across the media industry, setting new standards for verifying information and debunking falsehoods.

While the benefits of such partnerships are clear, they also present challenges, including the need for maintaining editorial independence and ensuring that technological solutions do not inadvertently suppress legitimate discourse. The sustainability of these collaborations often depends on securing ongoing funding and resources, highlighting the need for a commitment from all stakeholders to invest in the long-term health of the information ecosystem.

In the quest for truthful reporting, partnerships between media organisations, academic institutions, and technology companies offer a promising pathway. By pooling expertise and resources, these collaborations can develop effective tools and strategies to combat misinformation and foster a culture of accuracy and integrity in journalism. Drawing inspiration from successful international examples, Australia has the opportunity to pioneer innovative approaches to truthful reporting, contributing to a media environment that serves the public interest with unwavering support.

TRANSPARENCY IN POLITICAL ADVERTISING

Political advertising during election campaigns plays a central role in shaping public opinion and electoral outcomes. However, the potential for such advertising to mislead the public through false or deceptive claims poses a significant threat to the integrity of democratic processes. The issue of transparency in political advertising in Australia, as in many democracies, is fraught with complexities, balancing the sacrosanct principle of freedom of speech against the imperative to protect the electorate from misinformation. The challenge is to craft legislation that adequately guards against the dissemination of misleading information without unduly infringing on political discourse.

The comparison between the regulation of political advertising and the advertising of goods and services is particularly instructive. In the commercial field, advertisers are subject to stringent regulations designed to prevent misleading or deceptive conduct, with significant penalties for violations. The rationale for such regulations is clear: consumers make better decisions when they have access to accurate information. The same logic applies, even more compellingly, to the political sphere, where the stakes include not just individual consumer choices but the future direction of the country.

Australia's foray into regulating political advertising with the aim of ensuring accuracy—legislation enacted in 1984 and subsequently repealed before the 1987 election—highlights the contentious nature of this issue. The repeal of this legislation underscores the formidable challenges in defining "misleading" within the context of political discourse, enforcing regulations, and navigating the potential for such rules to be weaponised for partisan purposes.

Yet, the absence of robust regulations on political advertising has left a vacuum that too often is filled by misleading claims and hyperbole, contributing to public cynicism and distrust in the political process. The draft legislation introduced by the Labor government in 2023—aimed at enhancing transparency in political advertising—while a step in the right direction, has been criticised for lacking the strength and enforcement mechanisms necessary to be effective. This points to a broader dilemma: how to craft legislation that is both enforceable and respectful of free speech rights.

The challenge lies in delineating the boundary between legitimate political argument, which can involve subjective opinions and interpretations, and outright falsehoods or deceptions that have no factual basis. Stricter regulations on political advertising must therefore be carefully calibrated to target only those advertisements that are misleading in a demonstrable way, without stifling political debate and discourse.

One potential approach is to require clear disclosures about the sources of political advertisements and the factual basis of their claims. Such disclosures could help voters to better assess the credibility of the information presented and make more informed decisions at the ballot box. This transparency could be facilitated by a dedicated oversight body with the authority to review complaints, assess the veracity of political advertisements, and mandate corrections or retractions where necessary.

Looking internationally, countries like Canada, New Zealand and members of the European Union have implemented various measures aimed at increasing transparency in political advertising, including requiring disclaimers regarding sponsorship and funding, as well as establishing independent bodies to monitor and adjudicate complaints about misleading advertisements. These examples offer valuable lessons on balancing the need for regulatory oversight with the protection of political expression.

Developing effective legislation on political advertising transparency in Australia will require a multi-pronged approach, incorporating clear definitions of misleading content, mechanisms for rapid adjudication of complaints, and appropriate penalties for violations. Any such legislation should be complemented by broader efforts to enhance media literacy among the electorate, empowering voters to critically evaluate political information.

The task is undoubtedly complex, and the concerns about potential overreach and the suppression of free political expression are not unfounded. However, the cost of inaction—allowing misleading political advertising to erode the quality of democratic discourse and decision-making—is too high. Through a consultative process that involves political parties, civil society, and the public, Australia can develop a regulatory framework that strikes an appropriate balance, ensuring that political advertising serves to inform the electorate rather than mislead it.

SUPPORT FOR INVESTIGATIVE JOURNALISM

In the rapidly evolving media landscape, investigative journalism remains a beacon of hope for uncovering truths, holding power to account, and fostering a well-informed public. Yet in an industry that is more intent on 'infotainment' and volume of engagement rather than quality of engagement, the value of investigative journalism has been left behind, even though wherever it does appear, it is of an exceptionally high quality.

The critical role of investigative journalism in Australia has been underscored by its success in bringing to light significant issues such as child sexual abuse within churches, war crimes in Afghanistan, and the bugging scandal by the Australian government in East Timor. These examples highlight not only the societal value of investigative journalism but also the complexities and challenges associated with funding and supporting such endeavours in an era where legacy media faces significant financial difficulties.

The financial decline of traditional media outlets, driven by the shift of advertising revenues to digital platforms and changes in consumer behaviour, has led to budget cuts, downsizing, and in some cases, the closure of newsrooms. This economic pressure has particularly impacted the capacity for investigative journalism, which is time-consuming, resource-intensive, and inherently riskier than other forms of journalism.

Despite these challenges, the need for robust investigative journalism has never been greater, prompting a search for sustainable models of support and funding.

The debate between channeling support through established public broadcasters such as the ABC versus independent news funding mechanisms offers a glimpse into the potential pathways for sustaining investigative journalism. Each model presents its own set of advantages and challenges.

Public broadcasting model: The ABC, with its national reach and mandate to serve the public interest, is well-positioned to undertake investigative journalism projects, especially under its flagship program, *Four Corners*. Leveraging public funding, the ABC can allocate resources to in-depth investigations without the immediate pressure for commercial returns that constrain private media entities. However, reliance on government funding raises concerns about editorial independence, particularly in investigating stories that may be politically sensitive. Ensuring the ABC's autonomy from political influence is therefore paramount in this model.

Independent news funding: An alternative approach involves creating or strengthening independent funds and foundations dedicated to supporting investigative journalism outside the purview of public broadcasters. These entities can provide grants, fellowships, and resources to journalists and media outlets pursuing investigative projects. The advantage of this model lies in its potential to support a diverse array of voices and outlets, including smaller and independent media organisations that may lack the financial resources of larger entities. However, the sustainability of such funds and their ability to provide consistent support over time can be a challenge, especially if a benevolent financial supporter decides that the areas that are being investigated are not worthy of merit or, indeed, investigate areas that might present a conflict of interest.

Supporting investigative journalism in Australia in the face of financial challenges requires a multi-faceted approach that combines public funding, independent financial mechanisms, diversified revenue strategies, collaborative projects, and technological innovation. By fostering a supportive ecosystem for investigative journalism, Australia can ensure that critical stories of public interest continue to be told, contributing to a more transparent, accountable, and democratic society.

*

CHAPTER 6: CONSTITUTIONAL REFORM

Over time, there has been increasing recognition of the need to modernise the Australian Constitution to better align with the demographic shifts, evolving values, and technological advancements of 21st-century Australia, suggesting a disconnect between the historical document and the needs of contemporary society. While the task of updating or replacing the Constitution is daunting due to the stringent requirements for amendments and the complexity of the issues involved, various paths forward offer potential for significant and beneficial reform. The choice between drafting a new Constitution or amending the existing one will depend on the level of public and political appetite for change and the specific goals that proponents of reform aim to achieve.

MOVE TOWARDS A NEW AUSTRALIAN CONSTITUTION

The Australian Constitution, established in 1901, is a cornerstone of the nation's legal and governmental systems, yet it is famously difficult to amend, a rigidity primarily due to the stringent requirements for any proposed changes to be accepted and enacted.

At the heart of the amendment difficulty is the "double majority" rule, which stipulates that for any amendment to pass, it must not only gain the majority of votes across the entire country but must also secure the majority in a majority of the states. This means that an amendment needs the support of over half of the voters nationally and must be favoured by voters in at least four of the six states, a dual requirement that was designed to ensure a broad consensus across the diverse geographic and demographic landscape of Australia, protecting smaller states from being overpowered by the more populous ones.

The rationale behind such a stringent amendment process can be traced back to the drafting of the Constitution in the 1890s, where the framers were determined to create a stable and enduring framework that could unify a geographically vast and regionally diverse country under a single set of fundamental laws and principles. They sought to balance the power between the federal government and the states, ensuring that significant changes to the national legal structure required a substantial agreement reflecting both the majority of the population and the majority of the states.

However, this high threshold for amendments has significant implications. On one hand, it helps safeguard the Constitution from capricious or momentary shifts in public opinion, and provides a stable legal environment. On the other hand, it can inhibit necessary reforms and adaptations that could address contemporary issues effectively. For instance, changes that might be popular in larger states or nationwide might still fail if they do not garner enough support from smaller states, potentially leading to a lack of progress in critical areas like environmental law, Indigenous rights, or technological advancements.

The practical effects of this stringent amendment process are evident in the history of referendums in Australia. Since 1901, over 40 proposals have been put to a referendum, but only a few have been successful. This low success rate illustrates the challenge of achieving the broad-based consensus required under the double majority rule.

The difficulty in amending the Constitution also reflects deeper political and social dynamics within Australia, which often necessitates extensive negotiation and compromise between different political factions and regional interests, which in turn, can be a protracted and fractious process. The rigorous demands for amending the Constitution mean that significant legislative changes typically require careful preparation, widespread public consultation, and strong bipartisan support, which are not always possible.

HISTORICAL CONTEXT AND LIMITATIONS

The Australian Constitution, drafted in the late 19th century, was a product of its time, tailored to address the social, political, and economic conditions of the 1890s. This period was marked by a desire for federation among the Australian colonies, which sought to unify under a single constitution while still preserving substantial independence and powers for each constituent state. The constitution aimed to establish a federal system that balanced these diverse regional interests against the need for a coherent national policy.

Given the era in which it was crafted, the Australian Constitution incorporated prevailing values and understandings, which may now seem outdated in light of contemporary issues and societal norms. For example, the original document did not acknowledge Indigenous Australians, nor did it account for modern considerations such as environmental protection, digital privacy rights, or gender equality, nor did it include women in any of its considerations. These omissions reflect the limitations of the historical context in which the constitution was created—limitations that increasingly challenge its applicability to modern governance.

One of the principal challenges posed by these historical limitations is the constitution's inflexibility in adapting to societal changes without formal amendments. As societal values evolve and new challenges emerge, the static nature of the Constitution can hinder the country's ability to respond effectively. This rigidity is exacerbated by the stringent amendment process, which, as discussed previously, requires significant consensus across both the population and the states.

This historical context has significant implications for contemporary Australia. For instance, the constitution's failure to recognise Indigenous Australians or provide a framework for acknowledging their unique cultural, historical, and land rights has been a source of ongoing tension and debate. Similarly, issues such as climate change and digital surveillance are scarcely addressed, leaving gaps that must be filled by legislation, which can be less stable and more subject to political fluctuations than constitutional provisions.

The Constitution's framing in the 1890s has also influenced the political structures it established, such as the representation in the Senate. Designed to protect the interests of smaller states by giving them equal representation to larger ones, this system now poses questions about democratic equity and representation efficacy, as population disparities among states have grown significantly. For example, the population of Tasmania in 2023 was 573,300, whereas the population of Australia's largest state, New South Wales, was 8,394,700—almost fifteen times larger than Tasmania—yet both states elect twelve Senators each to the federal parliament. The Australian Capital Territory has a population of 469,200, fast approaching the population of Tasmania, yet it only elects two Senators to the federal parliament.

In addition, the economic structures and policies appropriate at the time of the Constitution's drafting do not necessarily accommodate the complexities of a globalised economy or the nuances of international trade and digital commerce. This mismatch can lead to inefficiencies and legal uncertainties that complicate Australia's economic policy and international dealings.

Despite these limitations, the Constitution has also demonstrated a remarkable degree of durability, providing a stable legal framework that has supported the country's development into a prosperous and democratic nation. However, the ongoing relevance of this foundational document is contingent upon its ability to evolve with Australian society and, it does not enable this level of flexibility. There needs to be a balance between preserving institutional stability and enabling necessary legal evolution to meet new challenges, and this can only be achieve through the creation of a new Constitution.

LOW SUCCESS RATE OF REFERENDA

The historically low success rate of referenda to amend the Australian Constitution is a telling aspect of its rigidity and the political landscape of Australia. Out of 45 attempts to amend the Constitution since its adoption in 1901, only eight have been successful, a success rate of 17 per cent. This pattern highlights not only the challenges inherent in the amendment process but also the complexities of political opposition that can arise, often stymieing changes regardless of their potential merits.

One of the primary reasons for the low success rate is the political opposition that amendments typically face, which can easily become entangled in partisan conflicts, where opposition parties may campaign against a proposal simply to weaken the governing party, regardless of the intrinsic value or necessity of the change. This political response is facilitated by the requirement for a double majority, which inherently demands wide-reaching consensus that spans both geographic and political lines—a tall order in any political climate.

The public's engagement with and understanding of constitutional matters can also affect referendum outcomes. Constitutional amendments often involve complex legal language and concepts that may not resonate with or be easily understood by the general populace. Without adequate understanding, voters may be inclined to vote conservatively to avoid unintended consequences, adhering to the adage, "if in doubt, vote no," a catchcry which was very potent in the Voice to Parliament referendum in 2023. This conservative approach to constitutional change is compounded by the fact that successful referendums often require extensive public education campaigns, which can be difficult to execute effectively.

The suggestion to develop a new Constitution and put it to a referendum to repeal the current one and implement a new framework introduces additional layers of complexity. Such a fundamental change would require not only vast political and public support but also a significant preparatory effort in terms of drafting, debate, and consensus-building akin to the constitutional convention of the 1890s. This convention would need to gather a diverse array of viewpoints and forge a consensus across Australia's varied political and social landscape—a formidable challenge given the current partisan divides and regional differences.

Achieving bipartisan support is crucial for any substantial constitutional reform. The history of successful amendments shows that those with clear bipartisan backing and less contentious provisions stand a better chance of acceptance. However, the process of garnering such support is intricate and fraught with potential for political loss, making parties wary of committing to a process with uncertain outcomes.

In addition to political and public consensus, a successful overhaul of the Constitution via a new referendum would likely depend on a period of stable government and economic conditions, allowing the public and politicians alike to focus on long-term structural changes rather than immediate concerns. This focus can be elusive in the context of electoral cycles and short-term political calculations.

While the idea of a new Constitution might seem appealing as a solution to the challenges posed by the existing one, the practicalities of achieving such a comprehensive reform through a referendum are daunting. The low success rate of past referenda underscores the difficulty of altering Australia's foundational legal document and suggests that any attempt to replace it entirely would require an unprecedented level of political skill, public engagement, and consensus-building.

A NEED FOR MODERNISATION

The call for modernizing the Australian Constitution resonates with increasing urgency as the gap widens between the static, century-old document and the dynamic realities of twenty-first-century Australia. This need for modernisation stems from fundamental shifts in demographics, societal values, and technological advancements, which the original document, anchored in the context of the 1890s, could scarcely anticipate.

Firstly, demographic changes have dramatically reshaped the social fabric of Australia. Over the decades, Australia has transformed into one of the most multicultural countries in the world, with significant immigration contributing to a diverse population. This demographic shift brings with it new perspectives and needs, which are not adequately reflected in the current constitutional framework. Issues such as multicultural representation, immigration policies, and non-discrimination are pressing yet underrepresented in constitutional discourse.

Additionally, societal values in Australia have evolved, with significant shifts towards greater inclusivity and recognition of rights for all citizens, including Indigenous populations and the LGBTQ+ community. The Constitution's silent stance on many of these issues means it often lags behind legislative changes and societal norms, necessitating a framework that can more readily adapt to and reflect contemporary Australian values.

Technological advancement is another critical area where the Constitution shows its age. The digital era has introduced complex issues related to privacy, data security, and the impact of technology on employment and personal freedoms. Current constitutional provisions offer scant guidance on these modern challenges, leaving gaps that are often filled by piecemeal legislation and judicial interpretation. A modernised constitution could provide foundational principles that guide the development of laws adapting to technological change, ensuring protections and frameworks that keep pace with innovation.

The need for flexibility in the Constitution is also paramount. The rigid amendment process, while designed to ensure stability and thorough deliberation, often acts as a barrier to timely and necessary updates. This inflexibility can hinder Australia's ability to respond effectively to emerging challenges and global shifts, putting the nation at a competitive and social disadvantage. More flexible constitutional mechanisms could include provisions for periodic review, enabling adjustments that reflect current realities without the need for cumbersome and uncertain referenda.

Environmental concerns, which have become increasingly prominent, illustrate another area where the Constitution falls short. Issues like climate change and sustainable development require integrated national responses, which are currently left to the legislative and executive branches without the constitutional backing that could ensure long-term commitment and coherence across government policies.

Modernising the Australian Constitution is not only a legal or procedural necessity but a fundamental requirement to align the nation's highest legal document with the lived realities of its people. This modernisation would involve not only adding new provisions that reflect current issues and values but also creating mechanisms within the document itself that allow for smoother, more responsive changes. Such a revitalised Constitution could better serve as a living document, evolving alongside the nation it governs, and providing a stable yet flexible framework that supports the growth and development of Australia into the future.

HOW THE AUSTRALIAN CONSTITUTION COMPARES INTERNATIONALLY

Internationally, constitutions vary widely in their mechanisms for amendment and adaptation. For example, the United States Constitution, also known for its rigidity, requires a two-thirds majority in both houses of Congress and ratification by three-quarters of the states to amend. Despite this, the U.S. has managed to amend its Constitution 27 times, a testament to a political culture that, at key moments, has supported foundational changes.

In contrast, more modern constitutions, like that of South Africa, adopted in 1996, incorporate mechanisms designed to facilitate easier amendments in response to changing societal needs. South Africa's constitution can be amended by a two-thirds majority in its National Assembly, reflecting a more flexible approach that recognises the necessity of evolving legal frameworks to address contemporary issues.

Similarly, the constitution of India provides a tiered amendment process where most amendments require a two-thirds majority in both houses of Parliament, but some changes, especially those affecting federal relations and fundamental rights, also require ratification by at least half of the state legislatures. This system, while ensuring stability, also allows for a degree of flexibility that the Australian system lacks.

Proponents of the rigidity of the Australian Constitution argue that it serves as a bulwark against hasty or ill-considered changes that could destabilise governance or undermine longstanding rights and freedoms. They value the stability and continuity it provides, which has undeniably contributed to Australia's democratic resilience and governance consistency.

However, while the Australian Constitution has served as a stable foundation for over a century, its comparative analysis with other global constitutions highlights its limitations in flexibility and adaptability. This rigidity may be increasingly at odds with the dynamic and fast-evolving nature of modern societal, technological, and global challenges. The debate over its suitability in contemporary times is thus not only about its capacity for change but also about balancing stability with necessary evolution to meet the demands of a twenty-first-century Australia.

RECOGNISE INDIGENOUS AUSTRALIANS AND THEIR UNIQUE RIGHTS

While the road to constitutional recognition and further rights for Indigenous Australians is fraught with challenges, it remains a crucial endeavour. The path forward involves not only legal and political changes but also a profound cultural shift in how Indigenous rights and history are understood and respected in Australia. Recognising Indigenous Australians in the Constitution and implementing further reforms such as a treaty or a Voice to Parliament are critical steps towards rectifying historical injustices and improving the lives of Indigenous communities. These proposals aim to acknowledge the distinct status and rights of Indigenous peoples as the first inhabitants of Australia.

CONSTITUTIONAL RECOGNITION

The issue of formally recognising Indigenous Australians in the Constitution has been a significant aspect of constitutional debates in Australia, highlighted during the referenda proposals of 1999 and 2023. These proposals aimed to amend the Constitution—the preamble, in the case of the 1999 referendum—to acknowledge the unique cultural, historical, and spiritual connections of Indigenous peoples to the land, an acknowledgment that not only seeks to rectify historical oversights but also to foster greater inclusivity and respect within the Australian legal framework.

The 1999 referendum was part of a broader set of proposals which, among other things, included the consideration of Australia becoming a republic. The specific proposal related to Indigenous

Australians aimed to insert a preamble into the Constitution that would recognise their special place in Australian history and society. However, the proposal was met with mixed reactions: critics argued that the preamble was merely symbolic and lacked any legal effect that would alter the lives of Indigenous Australians or provide any substantial rights or protections. Supporters believed that even symbolic recognition was a crucial step toward reconciliation. Ultimately, the referendum failed to pass, with 55 per cent of voters rejecting the republic proposal and 60 per cent rejecting the preamble. This outcome reflected a variety of factors, including political divisions, the complexity of the issues bundled together in the referendum, and a lack of consensus on the significance and implications of the proposed preamble.

Fast forward to 2023, and the debate took on new dimensions. This more recent proposal sought not only to recognise Indigenous Australians in a symbolic preamble but also aimed to introduce substantive constitutional changes through a Voice to Parliament. These included mechanisms for ensuring Indigenous voices could be heard in the legislative processes affecting them, such as through an advisory body that would be consulted on matters pertaining to Indigenous affairs. This move towards not only recognising the historical and cultural significance of Indigenous peoples but also providing a platform for their participation in governance was seen as a step towards substantive constitutional recognition.

The shift from a largely symbolic to a more substantive form of recognition reflects a deeper understanding of the needs and rights of Indigenous Australians. It acknowledges that true reconciliation and recognition involve more than mere acknowledgment; they require active and ongoing engagement with Indigenous communities to shape policies and decisions that affect their lives. This approach aimed to address the criticisms of the 1999 preamble proposal by embedding real mechanisms for inclusion and consultation within the constitutional framework.

The ongoing efforts to amend the Constitution to recognise Indigenous Australians underscore a broader movement towards recognising the rights and histories of Indigenous populations globally. Similar movements can be seen in other countries like Canada and New Zealand, where constitutional or legislative measures have been taken to recognise and incorporate Indigenous rights and perspectives into the national dialogue.

However, the challenges of achieving constitutional recognition of Indigenous Australians are significant. They involve not only the legal and political hurdles of amending the Constitution—as was discovered yet again in the 2023 referendum on the Voice to Parliament—but also the broader cultural and societal shifts required to support such changes.

The process requires building a consensus across diverse Australian communities and effectively communicating the importance and benefits of such recognition not only for Indigenous Australians but for the nation as a whole.

DEFEAT OF RECENT PROPOSALS

The defeat of the 2023 referendum on the Voice to Parliament—rejected by 60 per cent of the electorate and defeated in every state—marked a significant moment in the country's constitutional history, reflecting deep divisions within its society and the complex interplay of politics, race, and history.

One of the primary factors contributing to the defeat was the intense opposition from certain conservative groups, some of which infused the debate with racially charged rhetoric. This opposition often framed the proposal as one that would divide the nation along racial lines, suggesting that it would create a separate class of citizenship or confer special rights upon a segment of the population based on race. These arguments tapped into broader anxieties about identity and equity, pulling significant public sentiment against the proposal.

In addition, the campaign against the Voice to Parliament was marked by a significant misinformation effort, which clouded public understanding of what the Voice would entail and what its implications might be. Misconceptions and fears were stoked about the potential for the Voice to have veto powers over parliamentary decisions or that it would lead to legal fragmentation. Such misinformation underscored the challenges of conducting a nuanced and informed public debate on a constitutional issue that was already complex and laden with historical sensitivities.

The political landscape also played a critical role in the referendum's outcome. Unlike some past successful referendums, which had enjoyed broad bipartisan support, the 2023 proposal did not. The lack of unified political backing meant that the referendum was more vulnerable to being perceived through a partisan lens, with voters potentially aligning their views with those of their preferred parties rather than engaging deeply with the merits or drawbacks of the proposal itself.

The media's role in framing the debate also cannot be underestimated. Media coverage varied widely, with some outlets providing balanced, informative perspectives, while others clearly positioned themselves either for or against the referendum, sometimes echoing the racially charged narratives put forward by conservative opponents. This uneven media landscape likely influenced public perceptions and understanding, shaping the discourse in ways that did not always aid in a clear presentation of the facts.

Despite these challenges, the defeat of the referendum also reflects broader issues of trust and engagement between Indigenous communities and the wider Australian public. While many Indigenous leaders and groups strongly supported the Voice, seeing it as a step towards recognition and reconciliation, there remained a significant portion of the electorate that was either indifferent to or actively distrustful of such constitutional changes. This gap in trust and understanding speaks to ongoing challenges in Australia's journey towards reconciliation and equity.

THE CALL FOR A TREATY

The idea of a formal treaty between the Australian government and Indigenous communities has gained traction as an alternative to constitutional recognition, especially in the wake of the defeated 2023 referendum on the Voice to Parliament. This call for a treaty is rooted in a desire to address past injustices more comprehensively and to establish a structured framework for future relations between Indigenous peoples and the state. A treaty, unlike constitutional amendments or symbolic acknowledgments, could potentially provide a more concrete, actionable basis for reconciliation and mutual respect.

Treaties between Indigenous peoples and governments are not without precedent; several countries, including New Zealand with the Treaty of Waitangi and Canada with its numbered treaties, have engaged in such agreements. These treaties often aim to rectify historical wrongs by recognising the sovereignty and rights of Indigenous peoples, providing legal frameworks for land rights, self-determination, and cultural preservation.

In the Australian context, a treaty could serve several critical functions. First, it would provide formal recognition of the unique status and rights of Indigenous Australians, something that many advocates argue has been insufficiently addressed by existing legal and political frameworks. Such recognition could cover a range of issues, including land rights, preservation of language and culture, and Indigenous participation in governance.

Second, a treaty could establish a legal and practical framework for addressing specific grievances and challenges faced by Indigenous communities, such as disparities in health, education, and economic opportunities. By laying out clear obligations, commitments, and processes, a treaty could foster more systematic and structured efforts to close these gaps.

Third, negotiating a treaty could itself be an act of reconciliation, signaling a willingness on the part of the Australian government to engage directly and sincerely with Indigenous communities. The process of negotiation would need to be one of true partnership, involving substantial dialogue, mutual respect, and a willingness to confront uncomfortable truths about Australia's history and the ongoing impacts of colonisation.

However, as is the case with constitutional change, the path to a treaty is fraught with challenges. One of the primary obstacles is the diversity of Indigenous communities in Australia, which includes many different groups with distinct cultures, languages, and priorities. Achieving consensus among these groups about the goals and terms of a treaty could be a complex and time-consuming process.

But, most importantly, there is the question of political will: the process of negotiating and implementing a treaty would require sustained commitment from multiple governments over time, potentially spanning different administrations with varying levels of commitment to the treaty process. The political environment must be conducive to such a long-term engagement, which can be unpredictable.

Additionally, public support is crucial. Just as with constitutional recognition, the broader Australian public would need to be informed and supportive of a treaty for it to succeed. This requires comprehensive education and awareness campaigns to help non-Indigenous Australians understand the importance and benefits of a treaty, not only for Indigenous peoples but for the nation as a whole.

While a treaty represents a significant opportunity for advancing reconciliation and improving relations between Indigenous Australians and the state, it also poses substantial challenges. The feasibility and success of such a treaty will depend on the depth of commitment to the process from all parties involved, the ability to navigate complex and diverse needs, and the creation of a supportive political and social environment. If these conditions can be met a treaty could mark a crucial step toward healing and unity in Australia.

IS A VOICE TO PARLIAMENT STILL ACHIEVABLE?

The Uluru Statement from the Heart, which emerged from a national Indigenous constitutional convention in 2017, proposed the establishment of a Voice to Parliament—a mechanism intended to provide Indigenous Australians with a formal and more direct say in government policies and decisions affecting their communities. Following the defeat of the 2023 referendum to establish such a Voice, there are significant questions about the viability of future referenda on this issue and whether other methods could achieve similar goals.

The proposal for a Voice to Parliament was based on the premise that Indigenous Australians should have a greater role in the decision-making processes that impact their lives, which could lead to more effective, informed, and just policy outcomes, recognising the unique position and needs of Indigenous communities. The defeat of the referendum in 2023 did not negate the underlying issues that the proposal seeks to address but rather highlighted the complexities involved in gaining broad national consensus through the referendum process.

Considering the challenges of passing constitutional amendments via referenda, particularly those requiring the "double majority" that has made constitutional change in Australia so difficult, it is worth exploring whether there are alternative paths to achieve the goals envisioned by the Uluru Statement.

One alternative could be legislative measures. The government could enact laws to establish an advisory body similar to the proposed Voice, as has been the case in Victoria and South Australia. While such an approach would lack the constitutional entrenchment that a referendum would provide, making it less secure and more susceptible to change by future governments, it would also be more feasible to implement in the short to medium term. Legislative action could be tailored to create a framework for consultation and influence, though it would need robust safeguards to ensure its longevity and effectiveness.

Another approach could be the implementation of agreements between Indigenous communities and state or territory governments. These agreements could focus on local governance and regional decision-making, providing a more decentralised model that might be more immediately impactful for specific communities. Such agreements could also serve as a proving ground for the efficacy of enhanced Indigenous consultation, potentially building broader support for national initiatives in the future.

In addition, advocacy and public education campaigns could be intensified to build greater awareness and support for the principles behind the Voice. By increasing understanding among the broader population of the historical context and contemporary challenges faced by Indigenous Australians, proponents of the Voice could lay stronger groundwork for future constitutional or legislative efforts. However, as was the case during the 2023 Voice to Parliament, no amount of public education will be adequate if there is an inherent hostility to Indigenous issues within the electorate and within the mainstream media.

CHALLENGES IN MAINSTREAM ACCEPTANCE

The resistance to constitutional changes aimed at recognising Indigenous rights and addressing historical injustices in Australia can be deeply rooted in the nation's history, specifically the appropriation of land that began with British colonisation in 1788. This historical backdrop sets a complex stage for the acceptance of constitutional changes within mainstream Australian society, reflecting broader issues of racism and the acknowledgment of past wrongs.

The dispossession of Indigenous lands since the arrival of the British is a central trauma in the history of Indigenous Australians, entwined with ongoing disparities in health, education, economic opportunities, and representation. Despite these persistent issues, there remains significant resistance among some segments of the population towards fully acknowledging this history and its ongoing impact. This resistance is often influenced by a combination of historical amnesia, racism, and a reluctance to confront uncomfortable truths about Australia's past.

For many Australians, recognition of Indigenous rights and historical wrongs challenges foundational narratives about the nation's origins, development, and identity. The mythology of *terra nullius*—that Australia was land belonging to no one prior to British colonisation—was a legal and cultural assertion that has been difficult to dislodge from national consciousness. The 1992 Mabo decision by the High Court, which overturned this doctrine, marked a legal recognition of Indigenous land rights, but broader societal acceptance of what this means has been uneven.

Addressing this resistance is not merely a matter of changing laws or amending the Constitution; it requires a fundamental shift in societal attitudes and a broad-based acceptance of the legitimacy of Indigenous claims to rights and recognition. This involves educating the public about the true history of colonisation and its effects on Indigenous peoples—an education that must start from early schooling and continue through to national discourse.

Media plays a crucial role in shaping perceptions and attitudes and responsible journalism that provides accurate historical accounts and fair coverage of Indigenous issues can help in reshaping public opinion. Cultural representations that include Indigenous voices and stories can also contribute to a more nuanced understanding of the past and present realities of Indigenous Australians.

Leadership from political, community, and business leaders can also significantly influence public sentiment. Leaders who openly support constitutional recognition and the rectification of historical injustices can sway public opinion and reduce societal resistance. This leadership must be consistent and based on a genuine commitment to reconciliation and justice, rather than symbolic gestures.

Grassroots movements and Indigenous activism remain vital in pushing for change and keeping issues in the public eye and these movements can engage broader segments of the population through public demonstrations, partnerships with non-Indigenous groups, and effective use of social media to educate and mobilise supporters.

Genuine dialogues that involve listening to and learning from Indigenous communities about their experiences, needs, and aspirations can help build bridges. These dialogues should be inclusive, respectful, and designed to produce actionable outcomes that reflect a commitment to rectifying past wrongs and moving forward together. Only through a comprehensive and sustained effort can there be hope for fostering a broader understanding and acceptance of the need to address historical injustices and ensure that Indigenous Australians are recognised as equal partners in the nation's future.

THE INCLUSION OF INDIGENOUS PEOPLE IN OTHER CONSTITUTIONS

The inclusion of Indigenous peoples in national constitutions is a important issue globally, as many countries struggle with histories of colonisation and the ongoing marginalisation of Indigenous communities. In this context, the Australian Constitution's approach to Indigenous recognition stands in stark contrast to several other nations that have taken more proactive steps in integrating Indigenous rights and recognition into their constitutional frameworks.

Internationally, several countries have amended their constitutions or adopted new ones that explicitly recognise the rights and status of Indigenous populations, often in response to similar historical contexts as those found in Australia. These constitutional recognitions vary in form and substance but generally aim to address past injustices and lay a foundation for more equitable relationships.

For example, the Constitution of Bolivia, rewritten in 2009, is one of the most progressive in terms of Indigenous rights, recognising Bolivia as a multinational state and including extensive provisions on Indigenous autonomy, justice, and languages. This approach not only acknowledges the existence and rights of Indigenous peoples but also grants them significant power to govern themselves according to their traditional laws and practices.

Similarly, the Canadian *Constitution Act* of 1982 includes Section 35, which recognises and affirms the existing Aboriginal and treaty rights of Aboriginal peoples of Canada. This legal recognition provides a constitutional framework for the protection of cultural heritage and land rights, serving as a basis for numerous legal actions by Indigenous groups seeking to assert their rights.

In contrast, the Australian Constitution has no such provisions; Indigenous Australians are not explicitly recognised, and there are no entrenched protections for their rights or status. The lack of constitutional recognition reflects a significant gap in the formal acknowledgment of Indigenous Australians compared to countries like Bolivia and Canada, where constitutional changes have been part of broader movements toward reconciliation and justice for Indigenous peoples.

New Zealand offers another model through the Treaty of Waitangi, which, while not part of the formal constitution (New Zealand does not have a single codified constitution), serves a similar function. The Treaty, signed in 1840 between the British Crown and Māori chiefs, is considered a foundational document that guides legislation and government policy regarding Māori rights. Although disputes over the Treaty's interpretation and implementation continue, it provides a framework for engagement and redress that is lacking in the Australian context.

The difference in constitutional approaches is significant because it influences how Indigenous rights are protected and promoted within each country. In Australia, the absence of constitutional recognition means that Indigenous rights are primarily addressed through legislation and common law, which are more susceptible to change and less binding than constitutional provisions. This creates a less stable and secure environment for the protection of Indigenous rights, often leaving these rights vulnerable to political shifts.

Given these international comparisons, it becomes clear that Australia could consider several pathways for improving Indigenous recognition and rights protection. Options might include amending the constitution to include explicit recognition of Indigenous Australians and their rights, adopting a treaty similar to New Zealand's Treaty of Waitangi, or creating a multinational state framework similar to Bolivia's, tailored to Australian contexts and needs.

While various countries have taken steps to incorporate Indigenous recognition into their constitutions, Australia lags behind in this area, and there are many countries offering models from which Australia might be able to draw from in its ongoing debates and discussions about constitutional reform and Indigenous recognition.

IMPLEMENT AN AUSTRALIAN REPUBLIC

The debate over Australia transitioning to a republic involves significant constitutional and national identity considerations. The idea is to reflect Australia's sovereignty and maturity as an independent nation, moving away from its colonial past under British rule. While the push for an Australian republic has faced setbacks, ongoing public support suggests that the debate is still very relevant. Advancing this cause will require strategic discussions, educational outreach, and political cooperation to align public sentiment with constitutional change, ultimately allowing Australians to decide their country's head of state.

THE OBJECTIVES OF BECOMING A REPUBLIC

The movement toward transforming Australia into a republic centres on the primary objective of replacing the British monarch with an Australian head of state, reflecting a broader desire to affirm Australia's national identity and independence in the twenty-first century. The presence of the British monarch as the head of state is increasingly seen as an anachronism that does not align with the modern, diverse character of Australian society, nor does it adequately represent Australia's geopolitical position as a sovereign nation in the global community.

One of the primary arguments in favour of Australia becoming a republic is the enhancement of national identity. As Australia has grown and evolved, its cultural, demographic, and political landscapes have diversified significantly. A distinctly Australian head of state would serve as a symbol of this unique national character, embodying and promoting the values and aspirations of all Australians, rather than those inherited from a colonial past tied to Britain.

Becoming a republic is also seen as a completion of Australia's path to full sovereignty and independence. While Australia is an independent nation—this was confirmed through the creation of the *Australia Act* in 1986—the symbolic connection to the British monarchy can be perceived as a residual form of colonial oversight. Moving to a republican model would mark the final step in a long process of decolonisation, removing any remaining vestiges of British authority over Australian affairs. This change would likely strengthen Australia's sense of self-determination and empower it to engage on the international stage as a fully autonomous nation, making decisions that are seen both domestically and internationally as entirely its own.

In addition, transitioning to a republic could foster a greater sense of unity and inclusivity within Australia. The monarchy is sometimes viewed as representing a particular segment of Australian society—one with historical ties to Britain and European heritage. In contrast, a republic, with a head of state who is of and from the people, would be more reflective of Australia's multicultural population, including Indigenous Australians and immigrants from many different backgrounds. This inclusivity could reinforce social cohesion and national solidarity.

There is also a practical aspect to becoming a republic, related to the legal and political operations of governance. Having an Australian head of state could simplify constitutional and governmental processes by aligning them more closely with the realities of Australia's independent legal and political systems. It would remove any ambiguity about the role of the monarchy and the Governor–General—or a President—clarifying the functions and duties of Australia's highest offices and making the system more transparent and accountable.

The debate about becoming a republic often includes discussions about constitutional reform in broader terms. Transitioning to a republic provides an opportunity to reconsider and potentially revise other aspects of the Constitution that may be outdated or ineffectual. This could lead to a more comprehensive modernisation of Australia's constitutional and legal framework, allowing for reforms that better address contemporary issues and challenges.

Despite these arguments, the transition to a republic is a complex and contentious issue, requiring broad national consensus and careful consideration of the legal, political, and cultural ramifications. It would involve significant changes not only to the structure of the government but also to the national psyche and identity.

PREVIOUS REFERENDUM AND OUTCOME

In 1999, Australia held a referendum that sought to alter the nation's constitutional monarchy into a republic, essentially to replace the British monarch with an Australian head of state, marking a significant shift towards full national sovereignty. However, voters rejected the republic model presented and the outcome has been a subject of extensive analysis and debate, revealing a complex interplay of political, social, and ideological factors that contributed to the failure of the campaign.

The model proposed in the 1999 referendum was for a President to be appointed by a two-thirds majority of the Federal Parliament and the model was intended to preserve political stability by avoiding direct election of the head of state, which could potentially rival the authority of the Parliament and Prime Minister. However, the model became one of the central points of contention and is often cited as a key reason for the referendum's failure.

Critics of the model, including many from within the ranks of republic supporters, argued that it did not go far enough in democratising the head of state's role, where they felt that the model maintained excessive parliamentary control and lacked the direct democratic engagement of the Australian people in choosing their head of state. This division within the pro-republic camp led to a lack of unity and weakened the overall campaign.

On the political front, the referendum was significantly influenced by the incumbent Prime Minister, John Howard, a known monarchist who was accused of manipulating the referendum process to ensure its failure, and Howard's personal biases against the republic were evident in the way the referendum was framed and conducted. By proposing a model that was likely to divide republic supporters, and not endorsing the campaign vigorously, Howard ensured that even those in favour of a republic were not fully supportive of the model put to vote.

The leadership of the pro-republic campaign, led by the future prime minister, Malcolm Turnbull, also faced significant challenges. There was a clear inability among the campaign leaders to agree on a single, unifying model that could appeal broadly to the Australian public and it was this lack of consensus, combined with ineffective communication and campaign strategies, meant that the public received mixed messages about what the shift to a republic would mean for Australia.

As was the case with the 2023 Voice to Parliament referendum— and looking back further to history, the suite of referendum questions in 1988, where four very reasonable proposals were comprehensively defeated—the 'No' campaign capitalised on these divisions and uncertainties. They effectively played on fears of unwanted change and potential political instability, arguing that the existing system, while not perfect, provided a known quantity that safeguarded Australia's political stability. The 'No' campaign also painted the move to a republic as 'elitist' and unnecessary, framing it as a change that would benefit politicians more than ordinary Australians.

In retrospect, the 1999 referendum on the Australian republic was not only a legal or political event but also a profound moment of national reflection on identity, sovereignty, and the future direction of the country. The defeat of that referendum underscored the complexity of such a significant constitutional change and highlighted the need for greater unity, clearer communication, and more inclusive planning in future efforts towards becoming a republic. It also demonstrated that changing a nation's system of governance involves deep-seated beliefs and values that require careful consideration and respect in any campaign for change.

PUBLIC SUPPORT FOR A REPUBLIC

Despite the setback of the 1999 referendum, subsequent polls and studies have consistently shown that a significant portion of the Australian population supports the notion of the country transitioning to a republic. However, translating this support into a decisive push for constitutional change has proven challenging, largely due to a combination of public apathy, lack of interest, and the absence of a compelling narrative to mobilise the populace.

Public support for a republic in Australia appears to be broad but not deeply passionate. While many Australians might favour the idea of having an Australian head of state in theory, this support often does not translate into active advocacy or a strong desire to see immediate change. This paradox can be attributed to several factors that influence public engagement and the perceived urgency of the issue.

Firstly, apathy plays a significant role. For many Australians, the monarchy's role is largely symbolic and does not impact their daily lives and also feeds into a "if it ain't broke, don't fix it" sentiment. While the idea of a republic might be appealing, it is not seen as a pressing issue. This apathy is compounded by the perception that the current system, though anachronistic, is fundamentally stable and not harmful and, in a country with numerous pressing issues such as economic stability, healthcare, and environmental concerns, constitutional change can seem like a low priority.

The lack of a compelling, unifying narrative around the move to a republic also contributes to this apathy. Unlike other constitutional issues that might have clear, tangible impacts on people's rights or the nation's policy direction, the change to a republic is often framed primarily as a symbolic gesture rather than a necessity and the benefits of such a change are not always clearly articulated beyond the abstract ideas of national identity and independence.

The complexity of the issue also plays a role. Constitutional change is a daunting prospect, involving intricate legal processes and significant political coordination. The failed 1999 referendum highlighted the divisiveness of the issue even among republic supporters, who could not agree on the model for a new head of state, and this complexity can deter engagement from the general public, who may feel ill-equipped to understand or contribute to the debate. In addition, there is a generational divide in attitudes towards the monarchy and a republic. Older Australians, who are more likely to have a sentimental attachment to the monarchy and its traditions, are often less enthusiastic about the change. In contrast, younger Australians, who might be more open to redefining Australia's identity, tend to be less engaged in traditional forms of political activism and more focused on other social issues.

Finally, the absence of strong leadership advocating for the republic is a critical factor. Successful constitutional changes often require charismatic and persistent advocacy from prominent leaders who can articulate the benefits and rally public support. Since the 1999 referendum, there has been a noticeable lack of sustained leadership on this issue, also contributing to its stagnation on the national agenda. For the republican movement to gain momentum, it would require not only increasing public awareness of the tangible benefits of such a change but also fostering a more engaging and compelling narrative that can unite various segments of the population and reinvigorate the discussion on national identity and independence.

CHALLENGES IN REFERENDA

Transitioning Australia to a republic poses several significant challenges, influenced by the complexities of the referendum process, the political climate, and the nature of public campaigns, which can sometimes distort or manipulate the actual sentiments of the populace. The case of other countries like Barbados, which transitioned to a republic in 2021, offers insightful comparisons and potential strategies for Australia, though distinct differences in political and cultural contexts must be considered.

The political climate and referendum process: The success of referenda has historically been low due to the stringent requirements for change, where the need for a "double majority" sets a high bar. This process inherently demands broad consensus, which is challenging to achieve in a diverse and politically fragmented landscape—the political climate at the time of a referendum plays a critical role. If the political leaders and major parties are not united in support of becoming a republic, the chances of passing a referendum diminish significantly, as was evident in the 1999 referendum, where divisions even among republic supporters regarding the model of the presidency led to the failure of the proposal.

Campaign misrepresentation: The role of campaigns in shaping public opinion and the outcomes of referenda cannot be overstated. Campaigns for and against becoming a republic can employ tactics that may not always accurately represent the implications of the change. Misinformation, fear-mongering, or overly simplistic portrayals of the issues can skew public perception. Effective and honest communication is crucial but often challenging to maintain in heated political environments where stakes are perceived as high.

Comparative international experiences: Barbados provides a recent example of a successful transition from a constitutional monarchy to a republic. In November 2021, Barbados declared itself a republic, removing Queen Elizabeth II as its head of state. This move was achieved not through a public referendum but through parliamentary vote, reflecting a significant consensus among political leaders and a different methodological approach compared to Australia's referendum-dependent process. The transition of Barbados was marked by strong leadership provided by the Prime Minister Mia Mottley, coupled with clear communication about the national benefits of such a change, emphasising sovereignty and national pride, without significant opposition.

Lessons for Australia: The approach by Barbados suggests that strong and unified political leadership is essential for major constitutional changes. However, adopting a similar parliamentary path in Australia would be challenging given the constitutional requirements for referenda. Nevertheless, the Australian movement towards a republic could benefit from observing how Barbados managed to cultivate broad political and public support, focusing on building a compelling, positive narrative around national identity and the benefits of full sovereignty.

In addition, Australia might consider engaging more deeply with community-level discussions and educational initiatives to build grassroots support. By ensuring the populace is well-informed and actively engaged in the conversation, the potential for misrepresentation by opposition campaigns can be mitigated.

While Australia faces significant challenges in changing to a republic, lessons from countries like Barbados highlight the importance of unified political leadership and clear, honest campaigning. For Australia, overcoming the hurdles of the referendum process and the potential for campaign misrepresentation requires a concerted effort to foster a unified vision and a well-informed public, coupled with strategic leadership that can navigate the complex dynamics of national identity and constitutional change.

*

CHAPTER 7: REPRESENTATION AND DIVERSITY

The engagement of underrepresented groups in Australian politics is crucial, and mechanisms such as like quotas should be considered to enhance diversity in political representation. There are challenges in fostering an interest and understanding of politics among these groups and the aim is to rectify the disconnection between the public and the political system, ensuring that governance truly represents and engages all sections of society.

ENSURE ENGAGEMENT AND IMPLEMENT QUOTAS FOR UNDERREPRESENTED GROUPS

Within Australian politics, the implementation of quotas represent a significant mechanism aimed at rectifying disparities in political representation among various underrepresented groups. These measures, which seek to bolster the participation of women, Indigenous Australians, LGBTQI+ communities, migrants from non-English speaking backgrounds, individuals with disabilities, and other marginalised communities, have been subject to considerable debate and varying degrees of adoption among the major political parties.

Quotas, as a form of affirmative action, function by setting mandatory minimums for the inclusion of specific groups within candidate lists and political party structures. This approach aims to ensure a baseline level of representation that might otherwise not be achieved through conventional selection processes. The rationale behind this mechanism is not only to enhance diversity for its own sake but to correct historical and systemic imbalances that have prevented certain groups from participating fully in the political process.

The Australian Labor Party provides a notable example of quotas in action: in 1994, the party introduced a system of quotas for women, which was met with skepticism and derision from conservative quarters—and some men within the ALP—with critics arguing that quotas undermine meritocracy and could lead to the selection of candidates based more on their demographic characteristics than on their qualifications or capabilities. Despite these criticisms, the quota system has had a profound impact on the composition of the ALP over the past three decades. Today, the ALP has a gender balance that approximates parity, a stark contrast to the Liberal Party, which has been slower to embrace similar measures and consequently has only 30 percent women representatives—this is not only confined to federal politics, but a feature of the Liberal Party across all states and territories.

The ideological opposition to quotas within some factions of the Liberal Party underscores a broader philosophical debate about the best means to achieve equitable representation. Opponents of quotas argue that such measures can be paternalistic or tokenistic, potentially stigmatising those they intend to help by suggesting that such candidates cannot succeed without institutional intervention. On the other hand, proponents contend that without such measures, the pace of change is glacial and insufficient to address the entrenched inequalities that pervade the political landscape.

Despite the controversy, the effectiveness of quotas in altering the demographics of political representation is undeniable. The

Labor Party's experience illustrates that quotas can dramatically accelerate the process of gender diversification within political ranks, and far from being tokenistic, has resulted in the election of many excellent women candidates and inclusion in the Labor Caucus and cabinet, candidates who previously would have been excluded due to the historical institutional barriers that had always deterred women from entering politics. However, the success of quotas for other underrepresented groups requires a similar commitment to structural changes and an acknowledgment of the unique barriers faced by each group.

For instance, Indigenous Australians, migrants from non-English speaking backgrounds, and individuals with disabilities face unique challenges that may require tailored approaches beyond quotas. These could include targeted recruitment efforts, specialised support systems within parties, and public education campaigns to reduce stigma and raise awareness. Several factors contribute to the slow progress in funding for disability services and related political action in Australia. Since 1901, only two federal politicians—Graham Edwards and Jordon Steele-John—have been wheelchair users. Would disability services in Australia be significantly better today if disability advocates had been actively involved in the political system much earlier and if there had been more advocates in parliament? Indigenous people were excluded from the development of federation in the 1890s and were completely overlooked in the Constitution. Could a quota system for Indigenous people in 1901 have prevented many of the issues that exist in the twenty-first century?

While quotas are not a panacea for all forms of political underrepresentation, they offer a practical tool that, when implemented thoughtfully, can contribute significantly to making Australian politics more inclusive, and the experience of the ALP's quota system implemented in 1994 shows that it's a system that can work in the public interest.

DIVERSITY OF REPRESENTATION

Achieving a diverse political representation that mirrors the demographic composition of Australia remains a significant challenge. While the current federal parliament is the most diverse in the nation's history, it still falls short of truly reflecting the broader Australian community. This gap highlights the need for continued efforts and innovative initiatives to foster a more inclusive governance structure, particularly within political parties that have traditionally been resistant to change, such as conservative factions.

The challenge with conservative parties often lies in their ideological foundations, which tend to emphasise tradition and stability over the rapid transformation of societal structures, including those of political representation. However, even within these frameworks, there are potential initiatives that could encourage greater diversity without fundamentally conflicting with their core principles.

While it could be seen as naïve to suggest this, one such initiative could be the adoption of more transparent and open candidate selection processes, and conservative parties—Liberal and National parties— could benefit from implementing systems that allow a broader base of party members to participate in the selection of candidates. This democratisation of the process could help to surface a more diverse array of candidates by reducing the influence of traditional power brokers who may favour candidates who resemble the existing political elite. Another approach could involve partnerships with community organisations that work closely with underrepresented groups. By collaborating with these organisations, conservative parties can gain deeper insights into the barriers that prevent diverse candidates from emerging within their ranks. These partnerships can also serve as a bridge to communities that may feel alienated from or skeptical of conservative politics, building trust and understanding that can facilitate more inclusive representation.

Mentorship and sponsorship programs within the parties could also be improved and play a crucial role. Established party members could take on mentorship roles for aspiring politicians from underrepresented backgrounds, providing guidance, exposure, and advocacy. This not only aids in the professional development of diverse candidates but also helps integrate them into the networks and structures that are essential for political advancement.

All political parties could consider setting internal targets for diversity—these are not rigid quotas but rather goals that aim to increase representation gradually. Such targets, coupled with regular reviews of progress and transparency in reporting, can create momentum and accountability within the party structure without imposing the kind of top-down mandates that quotas represent.

Educational initiatives are also vital. Educating party members about the benefits of diversity in political representation—not just in ethical or social terms, but also in enhancing the party's ability to govern effectively—can change perceptions from within. By highlighting how diverse perspectives can contribute to more robust decision-making and policy development, political parties—especially the conservatives—can foster a more accepting and proactive attitude towards inclusivity.

CHALLENGES IN POLITICAL ENGAGEMENT

Increasing and improving political engagement in Australian politics presents a range of challenges, particularly as it pertains to the apathy and disconnection that many citizens feel towards the political system. Understanding the roots of this disengagement and devising strategies to counter it are crucial for the health and effectiveness of democratic governance.

One fundamental challenge is the perceived irrelevance of politics to daily life. Many Australians, especially among younger and marginalised groups, feel that political discourse and decisions do not reflect their concerns or impact their everyday experiences. This perception leads to a lack of interest in participating in political processes such as voting, attending town hall meetings, or following political news.

To counter this, there needs to be a concerted effort to make politics more relevant and accessible to the general public. This could be achieved by ensuring that political communication is clear, straightforward, and directly addresses the concerns of diverse community segments. Politicians and parties must strive to speak in language that resonates with different groups, avoiding jargon and abstract policy descriptions that fail to illustrate the tangible effects of political decisions.

Another significant barrier is the distrust in politicians and the political system. This distrust is often fueled by scandals, corruption, and a lack of transparency in how decisions are made and implemented. To rebuild trust, stringent measures against corruption must be enforced, and greater transparency must be instituted across all levels of government. Implementing policies such as open meetings, public access to government documents, and strong accountability mechanisms can help reassure the public that their leaders and the system are working in their best interests.

The complexity of the political system itself can also be daunting for many citizens, and the structure of Australian government, with its multiple layers and functions, can be confusing. Simplifying the way political information is presented and educating the public about how government functions are essential steps in demystifying political processes and encouraging greater engagement. Educational programs that focus on civic literacy, starting from a young age and extending into adult education, can empower citizens to participate more fully in their democracy.

Additionally, the role of media in shaping political engagement cannot be underestimated. Often, media coverage of politics focuses on conflict and scandal, or the theatrical antics of Parliamentary Question Time, rather than substantive issues or the everyday workings of government and this often exacerbates public cynicism and fatigue with politics. While this might seem to be a tall order, encouraging or legislating media to engage in responsible reporting that emphasises informative content, diverse viewpoints, and constructive debates can help increase public interest and understanding of political matters.

Engaging underrepresented groups in politics often requires specific outreach and support initiatives. For instance, providing resources and platforms for these groups to voice their specific concerns can lead to greater involvement. Political parties and civic organisations might also develop targeted programs to identify and nurture potential leaders from underrepresented backgrounds, offering training and support to help them become effective advocates and politicians.

Improving political engagement in Australia is a multifaceted challenge that requires addressing the roots of apathy and disconnection, and this is an issue that only be addressed in the medium-to-long-term period: it will take time. By making politics more relevant, rebuilding trust, simplifying the political system, promoting responsible media coverage, and directly engaging with underrepresented communities, the gap between the public and the political system can be narrowed. This is crucial not only for the health of Australian democracy but also for ensuring that it remains responsive and representative in an increasingly complex and diverse society.

HISTORICAL CONTEXTS FOR CIVIC AND POLITICAL ENGAGEMENT

Has there ever been a 'golden age' of political engagement in Australia? There was certainly greater involvement and interest in politics during the time of the war with Vietnam in the 1960s, and there a strong interest in the acts of genocide in Ukraine and Gaza perpetrated by the Russian and Israeli governments, respectively. Certain events such as the dismissal of the Whitlam government in 1975 and the 2003 'weapons of mass destruction' debacle in Iraq have also piqued the interest large sections of the Australian population but have there been periods characterised by particularly high levels of political involvement and enthusiasm among the populace? This is vital in understanding the dynamics of political participation over time and in assessing whether current levels of political engagement are unprecedentedly low or part of a longer trend of fluctuating interest.

Australian political engagement has seen varied phases, influenced by both local and global events, social changes, and evolving political ideologies. From the early days of federation in 1901, through to the world wars, the post-war boom, and into the contemporary era, the level of political engagement has often mirrored the societal, economic, and cultural shifts occurring in and around Australia.

In the early twentieth century, following federation, there was a notable enthusiasm for politics as Australians navigated their new identity as a federated nation. The introduction of compulsory voting in 1924 was a significant development, ensuring high voter turnout and arguably reflecting a committed, if legally mandated, engagement with political processes. This period could be seen as a form of 'golden age', not necessarily because of voluntary enthusiasm for politics, but because of the high levels of participation that compulsory voting ensured. However, the concept of a true 'golden age' might be more myth than reality. While certain events, such as the reforms of the Whitlam era in the 1970s or the economic transformations under the Hawke and Keating governments in the 1980s and 1990s, sparked intense political interest and activity, these were often reactions to crises or transformative changes rather than indicators of sustained high engagement.

Other forms of political activism has played a crucial role throughout Australian history, with movements such as the labour rights campaigns in the early 20th century, the Indigenous rights movement, which gained significant momentum in the 1960s with the 1967 referendum, and the environmental activism prominent in the 1980s and beyond. These movements indicate periods of heightened political engagement among specific population segments, driven by a desire for change.

However, there has also been a consistent theme of disenchantment and disengagement of politics among many Australians. Factors contributing to this include the perception of politics as distant or irrelevant, disillusionment with the political class, and a sense that individual action is ineffective within the larger political framework. The rise of political cynicism can be traced back to multiple points in Australia's history where the public's expectations of political leaders went unmet—quite often, unreasonable expectations—leading to periods of significant disengagement.

In recent decades, the advent of the internet and social media has transformed political engagement, making it easier for people to access information, mobilise, and express their opinions. While this has led to new forms of engagement, such as digital activism, it has also contributed to the spread of misinformation and increased polarisation, complicating the landscape of political participation.

Political participation among the electorate has ebbed and flowed in response to various factors, and contemporary challenges in political engagement may be seen as the latest phase in this ongoing fluctuation rather than a new or unique phenomenon. Understanding this historical context needs to be taken into account in addressing today's challenges in political engagement and working towards a more inclusive and responsive democratic system.

IMPROVE YOUTH ENGAGEMENT IN AUSTRALIAN POLITICS

There needs to be a focused approach towards enhancing youth engagement in Australian politics through targeted policies, educational integration, and possible reforms such as lowering the voting age. These efforts aim to cultivate a politically active youth population that feels both empowered and represented within the political arena, thereby nurturing a generation that is well-informed and engaged in shaping their society.

The promotion of youth-friendly policies in Australia represents a strategic approach to enhancing political engagement among young people, a demographic that often feels disconnected from the traditional political process, and a group that is often dismissed by politicians or condescended to. By developing and advocating for policies that directly address the interests and needs of the youth, political parties and governments can cultivate a deeper interest in and commitment to the political landscape among this crucial segment of the population.

Youth-friendly policies encompass a broad range of topics that resonate with younger Australians, including education, employment, climate change, housing, digital innovation, mental health, and social justice. These issues are not only significant in the daily lives of young people but also play a crucial role in shaping their future prospects and quality of life.

To effectively promote youth-friendly policies, a multifaceted approach is needed. First, there must be a genuine commitment to understanding the unique perspectives and concerns of young people. This can be achieved through direct dialogue and sustained engagement with youth communities. Forums, workshops, and social media platforms offer valuable venues for politicians and policymakers to interact with young people, gaining insights into their views and priorities.

Involving young people in the policymaking process is also essential and this can be facilitated through the promotion of youth advisory councils, which can work alongside local and national government bodies to ensure that the voices of young people are heard and considered in legislative processes. Such councils can serve as a bridge between the government and the youth, providing a formal mechanism through which young individuals can contribute to governance.

Political parties and leaders should also focus on transparent and accessible communication to make politics more approachable for young people. This involves not only the content of the policies but also how they are communicated. Utilising digital platforms to disseminate information and engage with young voters can make political content more accessible and engaging, and social media, online forums, and interactive websites can serve as dynamic tools for presenting policy proposals and soliciting feedback from young audiences.

In addition to these direct engagement strategies, education plays a critical role in promoting youth-friendly policies. Incorporating comprehensive civic education into school curricula from an early age can equip young people with the knowledge and skills necessary to understand and engage with political issues. Education programs should cover the structure of government, the electoral process, the importance of voting, and how individual actions can influence political outcomes and this educational foundation can foster a sense of civic duty and empower young people to participate actively in politics.

The promotion of youth-friendly policies must be backed by real action. Policies need to be implemented effectively and their impacts regularly assessed and communicated, and success stories and positive outcomes should be highlighted to demonstrate to young people that their involvement in politics can lead to tangible changes. This not only reinforces the value of their engagement but also builds trust between young citizens and political institutions.

Youth engagement in politics can be further enhanced by lowering barriers to political entry, which could include lowering the voting age, to allow younger people a say in their governance earlier. It could also mean offering more support for young candidates who wish to enter politics, providing them with the resources and mentorship needed to navigate the political arena.

By promoting and implementing youth-friendly policies effectively, Australian political leaders and institutions can foster a more engaged, informed, and proactive youth populace. This not only benefits the youth directly but also enriches the democratic process, ensuring that it remains vibrant, responsive, and inclusive for future generations.

ENGAGEMENT THROUGH EDUCATION

Encouraging political engagement through education is a fundamental strategy for fostering a well-informed and participatory citizenry. By integrating political education and engagement into the curricula of schools and universities, we can begin to cultivate a connection to politics from an early age, shaping a generation that is both aware of and active in the democratic processes that affect their lives.

The basis for this educational approach is the belief that a deep understanding of political systems, civic responsibilities, and the rights of citizens is essential for the health of any democracy. By informing students about the integral relationship between the parliamentary system and the electorate, educational institutions can lay the groundwork for lifelong political engagement.

Starting in primary schools, the curriculum can include basic concepts of democracy and citizenship. While many schools include some of these areas within their curriculum, quite often, it involves a day visit to Parliament House, witnessing the antics of Question Time—a certain turnoff for many primary school students—and then never returning again to any of these matters, unless it's for the students who specifically choose a pathway through legal or political studies. These early educational experiences are crucial as they set the stage for more detailed study in later years and help to normalise political participation as an integral part of citizenship.

As students progress into secondary education, the curriculum can expand to cover more complex topics such as the electoral processes, the significance of the Constitution, the role of political parties, and the importance of civic engagement in maintaining a democratic society. Discussions and debates on current events can be encouraged to develop critical thinking skills and to connect theoretical knowledge with real-world situations. This phase of education should also emphasise the diversity of political thought, fostering an environment where different opinions are respected and debated.

Universities have a particularly potent role in political education, serving as hubs for advanced study and discussion of political theory, policy analysis, and governance. Most universities have devolved into corporatised sites solely based on learning, rather than also social engagement and interaction, or encouragement for students to participate in campus life and activities.

Cost of living issues, and financial pressures and burdens placed upon students means that many rely on multiple part-time jobs to support their studies, and have little time for extracurricular campus activities or engagement in university politics.

Ultimately, fostering political engagement through education requires a comprehensive, sustained approach that starts early and continues through to higher education. By providing students with the knowledge, skills, and motivation to engage in politics, educational institutions play a crucial role in maintaining and strengthening the democratic fabric of society. This educational foundation not only prepares students to be active participants in politics but also empowers them to be informed voters and potential leaders who can contribute to the ongoing development and improvement of their communities and country.

LOWERING THE VOTING AGE

The consideration of lowering the voting age in Australia presents a significant debate about the role of young people in democratic processes and their capacity to influence policies that will shape their future. The idea of reducing the voting age to 16, potentially on a non-compulsory basis, offers a radical yet increasingly discussed approach to enhancing civic engagement among youth and recognising their stake in political outcomes.

Lowering the voting age is not without precedent. Several countries have already taken steps to include younger individuals in the voting process. For example, Austria, Brazil, and Scotland allow 16-year-olds to vote in certain elections. These instances provide valuable case studies for the impact of such changes on political engagement and the overall democratic process. In Austria, after the voting age was lowered in 2007, studies found that 16- and 17-year-olds were just as likely as older voters to participate in elections, challenging the notion that younger people lack the interest or capacity to engage in political decisions.

The arguments in favour of lowering the voting age in Australia hinge on several key points. Proponents assert that young people at 16 are already engaging with complex societal issues through their education, are capable of employment, and are subject to various laws and taxes; hence, they should have a right to vote on the policies that affect these aspects of their lives. Additionally, allowing younger people to vote could lead to earlier and stronger habits of civic participation, fostering a more politically engaged populace over the long term.

Lowering the voting age to 16 could also serve as a catalyst for more youth-friendly policies. Politicians, recognising the electoral power of these young voters, might be more inclined to address issues such as climate change, education, and employment—topics that are of high priority to the younger demographic. This shift could lead to legislation that is more reflective of the needs and concerns of a broader section of the community.

However, there are also concerns and challenges associated with this proposal. Skeptics question whether 16-year-olds have the maturity and understanding necessary to make informed voting decisions and argue that many young people at this age have not yet had enough life experience or education in political systems to participate effectively in elections. But how does this compare with the 50-year-old who has no interest in politics or the issues that relate to the electorate, and despises turning up to the polling booth to vote every three years?

The implementation of a non-compulsory voting option for 16- and 17-year-olds could address some of these concerns by allowing those who feel ready and interested to participate without compelling all young people to vote before they feel equipped to do so. This approach could strike a balance between empowering enthusiastic young voters and not overwhelming those who may not yet have an interest or understanding of political affairs.

Lowering the voting age in Australia to 16, while making it non-compulsory, offers a promising avenue to empower young people and involve them more directly in the democratic process. The success of similar policies in other countries provides a compelling argument for its potential effectiveness. While such a significant change requires careful consideration, it does offer further enhancements to the civic education framework to ensure young voters are well-prepared to take part in shaping their society through the ballot box.

ADDRESS THE LACK OF INTEREST IN AUSTRALIAN POLITICS AND CIVIC INSTITUTIONS

A lack of interest in politics and civic institutions is consistent throughout Australia, which is consistent with trends in other Western democracies. Most voters prioritise government competence and effectiveness in addressing community needs over active political engagement. The question of how Australia compares with other nations in terms of civic engagement remains open, suggesting a need for further research into comparative political behaviour and societal attitudes towards governance.

The phenomenon of widespread disinterest in Australian politics, and in many other Western democracies, is a complex issue rooted in cultural, systemic, and individual factors. While this disengagement is not unique to Australia, the specific contours of Australian society—including its history of immigration and diversity—add unique layers to the general patterns of political apathy observed globally.

Many Australians feel that the decisions made in parliament have little direct impact on their daily activities and immediate concerns and the result is a feeling that politics is something conducted by elites within the confines of parliament, rather than as a participatory and impactful aspect of everyday life.

The legacy of migration also plays a significant role in shaping attitudes towards politics among certain segments of the Australian population. Many migrants to Australia have come from countries where political engagement was either not possible due to authoritarian regimes, or where it was fraught with danger and linked to human rights abuses. For these individuals, the stability and relatively benign nature of Australian politics, while a relief, may also diminish the perceived necessity of active political involvement.

In many countries around the world, political choices or political engagement can be a matter of life or death and in many cases, the wrong choice or acting against the prevailing political orthodoxy can result in imprisonment and human rights abuses. For many Australian residents who have directly arrived from these countries with oppressive regimes, or descend from these countries, there is a sense of contentment with a system that functions without their direct involvement, leading to a passive engagement with political processes.

The media also significantly influences public interest in politics. Sensationalist reporting and a focus on political scandals or confrontations can lead to cynicism and fatigue among the public, and this type of coverage often overshadows substantive policy discussions and diminishes the perceived integrity of political figures and institutions. Over time, this can erode trust in the political system and reduce the motivation to engage with politics beyond the sensational headlines.

The structure of the political system itself can also deter engagement. The dominance of major parties and the electoral system can sometimes create a sense of inevitability about election outcomes, leading to feelings of disenfranchisement among voters whose preferences do not align with the majority. This is particularly acute in systems where compulsory voting is in place, as in Australia, where disenchanted voters may participate out of legal necessity rather than genuine engagement, further perpetuating a cycle of disinterest.

Ultimately, tackling widespread disinterest in politics requires a multifaceted approach that addresses both the structural barriers to engagement and the cultural and perceptual factors that distance individuals from the political sphere. By making politics more accessible, relevant, and responsive, it is possible to reinvigorate engagement and strengthen the democratic process in Australia and other Western democracies.

VOTER EXPECTATIONS

In Australia, voter expectations significantly shape the interaction between the electorate and government officials. A predominant expectation among voters is the desire for a government that is competent and not corrupt, capable of addressing community concerns with efficiency and integrity, managing the economy effectively and efficiently, and providing opportunities for the populace in health, education and community engagement. This perspective indicates a preference for stability and efficacy in governance, often over and above the dynamics of active political participation or deep engagement with the political processes.

The preference for competency and honesty in government reflects a pragmatic approach to politics commonly found among Australian voters and many citizens are primarily concerned with outcomes rather than the intricacies of political machinations and interpersonal gamesmanship and ego. They expect the government to deliver essential services, ensure economic stability, maintain public safety, and uphold a standard of living that matches Australia's high global standing. As long as these basic expectations are met, a significant portion of the electorate does not feel the need to engage deeply with political processes or to alter their voting behaviours dramatically.

This set of expectations aligns with a broader trend towards technocratic governance, where the technical and managerial skills of leaders and their ability to effectively administer public policy are valued more highly than their ideological positions or charismatic appeal. In this context, voters are less likely to tolerate incompetence or corruption, as these directly undermine the ability of the government to meet its primary function—serving the public effectively.

However, this focus on competency does not necessarily imply an apathetic or disengaged electorate. Instead, it suggests that Australian voters have a specific set of criteria by which they judge their leaders, prioritising tangible results over political rhetoric. This pragmatic outlook means that political leaders are often under considerable pressure to perform and to demonstrate their administrative capabilities. It also means that when scandals or instances of incompetence arise, they can quickly erode public trust and lead to significant backlash, as voters feel their fundamental expectations are not being met. The former Prime Minister Scott Morrison was ultimately deemed to be incompetent and oversaw a government that engaged in too much corruption and was voted out of office in 2022: however, it has to be remembered that he did hold the confidence of the electorate and won the 2019 federal election. Which event was the true reflection of the electorate's adjudication of the Morrison government?

The implications of this focus on competency are significant for how political campaigns are conducted and how policies are presented to the public. Politicians and parties must highlight their achievements and competencies in practical, understandable terms that resonate with the daily lives of Australians. Policy proposals are often scrutinised not just for their visionary qualities but for their feasibility and the track record of those who will implement them. This voter attitude also impacts the accountability mechanisms within Australian politics. Since the electorate values competency and despises corruption, there is strong support for robust mechanisms to ensure transparency and integrity in governance. This includes support for independent watchdogs, strict regulations on lobbying and political donations, and comprehensive audits and reporting requirements for government projects.

In terms of policy direction, the government's focus tends to be on areas that directly impact the economic and social wellbeing of its citizens. This includes investments in healthcare, education, infrastructure, and security—areas where government competency is highly visible and directly felt by the public. As a result, political debates often centre around these key areas, with each party attempting to prove that they can manage them more effectively than their opponents.

Leaders are expected to govern well, rather than just talk well, and they are held accountable to these expectations through both electoral processes and established mechanisms of transparency and integrity. This dynamic ensures that even if deep political engagement is not widespread, the governance itself remains closely aligned with the core concerns and values of the Australian public.

COMPARISON WITH OTHER COUNTRIES

The phenomenon of disinterest in civic affairs and politics, while pronounced in Australia, is not a uniquely Australian issue but reflects a broader trend observable across many countries, particularly in Western democracies. A comparative analysis of civic engagement levels across different national contexts reveals a variety of factors that contribute to this widespread political apathy, as well as some unique approaches countries have taken to address it.

In the United States, for example, voter turnout and general political engagement have historically fluctuated significantly, influenced by various social, economic, and political factors, although the 62 per cent turnout of the voting-age population at the 2020 Presidential election was the highest recorded since the 1960 election. Similar to Australia, American voters often express a desire for competent governance and show a significant disdain for perceived corruption or inefficiency. However, unlike Australia, the U.S. does not have compulsory voting, which results in lower voter turnouts and arguably greater disengagement among the population. This difference underscores the impact of electoral systems on civic engagement, where mandatory participation can at least ensure higher physical turnout, if not always reflective of deeper civic involvement.

In contrast, Scandinavian countries such as Sweden, Denmark, and Norway exhibit high levels of political participation. These nations are often characterised by strong welfare states and a high degree of trust in public institutions, which correlates with greater civic engagement. Their political systems encourage active participation through proportional representation and extensive welfare policies that keep the electorate invested in the workings of government. This suggests that trust and perceived efficacy of the government play crucial roles in motivating political engagement.

Meanwhile, in countries like the United Kingdom, disengagement has been particularly evident among younger demographics, attributed to a sense of alienation from traditional political parties and the feeling that politics does not address their concerns, particularly around issues like housing and employment. The turnout at the 1950 British election was 84 per cent, whereas at the 2019 election, this number was down to 67 per cent. The Brexit referendum in 2016, however, saw a spike in political interest—a voter turnout of

72 per cent—demonstrating that high-stakes issues can temporarily re-engage disenchanted segments of the population.

In newer democracies, such as in Eastern Europe, political engagement has also been a mixed bag. Post-communist countries have struggled with both high levels of cynicism towards politics, due to historical distrust of government, and periods of intense political activism, as citizens exert their newly found democratic rights.

This international panorama shows that while disinterest in politics is widespread, the factors influencing it and the levels of engagement vary significantly across different political, cultural, and economic contexts. The effectiveness of the government, the level of corruption, the type of electoral system, the historical context, and the socio-economic environment all play critical roles in shaping civic engagement.

To improve civic engagement, countries have experimented with various strategies. These include reforming electoral systems to ensure more representative outcomes, implementing civic education programs to increase political literacy, and leveraging technology to better involve citizens in political processes. Social media and digital platforms, for example, have become new arenas for political discussion and activism, potentially engaging younger demographics who are traditionally less interested in formal political processes.

The disinterest in civic affairs and politics in Australia reflects a common challenge faced by many countries and each nation's specific context determines the extent and nature of political engagement. Understanding these global patterns can provide valuable insights into how to better foster civic participation and address the underlying causes of political apathy, ensuring that democracies remain robust and representative.

*

EPILOGUE: FIXING AUSTRALIAN POLITICS

NAVIGATING CHANGE, CHALLENGING POWER, AND EMBRACING A NEW VISION FOR THE FUTURE

Australia has undergone significant changes since federation, a development that is both evident and expected. The concerns, passions, attitudes, opinions, and worldview of the Constitution's authors differ greatly from those prevalent today. Some of their views might now be considered outdated or even offensive by much of the Australian population. The authors anticipated the need for change and provided mechanisms for it. Much of this change has been interpretive, particularly in terms of defining rights. The High Court has determined that the Constitution implies certain rights. Although the architects of the Constitution would likely agree with this principle, the specific rights they envisioned as covered might differ significantly from those recognized by the High Court today.

The Constitution, as we have observed, still exhibits significant shortcomings. The lack of Indigenous recognition, which notably failed to pass in the 2023 referendum, is a crucial amendment necessary for a modern nation. Another important transition is moving away from a monarchical system. Currently, we are witnessing turmoil within the Royal Family. The death of the widely beloved, if not universally so, Queen Elizabeth II has shaken the family, and the unpopularity of her heir, King Charles III—who is also dealing with health issues—highlights the institution's urgent need for modernisation. Part of this modernisation should involve removing the monarchy's role from the Australian Constitution and replacing it with a fair and democratic system.

One of the rights we have is freedom of religion. Of course, it is wrong to prevent or oppress the practice of religion, provided that its tenets do not violate the laws of the land. Most religions easily meet this criterion. However, while Australia is a secular nation with no official religion, certain religious leaders exert excessive influence on the Australian government. Personal faith as a foundation for one's ethical and spiritual beliefs is one thing; using religious beliefs to further the advantages of a select few is wrong and should be addressed accordingly.

Australia is a cautious and somewhat incurious nation, especially after many years of reform from 1972 to 2007, which have left the population apprehensive about further changes. A significant factor is that much of the surviving reform has not been beneficial to the vast majority of citizens. In addition, we have seen a resurgence of more traditional values—not necessarily desirable ones—that date back to 1788. Multicultural Australia is currently under siege by some who dislike immigration, even as they exploit migrants in employment, housing, health, and education. What is sorely needed is leadership that promotes genuine acceptance, not just 'tolerance'.

The party system is partly to blame for these issues. Major parties are built on structures from the nineteenth and twentieth centuries and a decline in party membership is one symptom of this outdated framework. Community engagement has evolved, and the traditional base of political parties—ranging from the lower middle class to the upper middle class—either no longer exists or has shifted its priorities. This decrease in membership makes it challenging for minor parties to survive; to be eligible to run in an election, a party needs 1,500 signed-up and verified members. For a small party, this requirement is extremely difficult to meet, and some have lost their status due to audits that may have miscounted members, missing the mark by only a few. While larger parties may meet the quota, the disinterest or lack of time among members means that the majority of the work falls on a few unappreciated volunteers, and this situation leads to candidate preselection issues. Smaller branches may find that head office parachutes outsiders in, posing a challenge for party membership to convince the local electorate to support them.

Party reform is another essential component needed to address issues in Australia. There are too many poor candidates in Parliament—members with no interest in the legislative process or the responsibilities of being a member of parliament. Many are incompetent, behave inappropriately, or are corrupt and venal. This isn't a new problem; such individuals have been part of Westminster Parliaments since 1688, but never before in such numbers or with such prominence. It is no coincidence that recent Australian Parliaments have been substandard: the preselection of too many unfit candidates and their subsequent promotion have had serious repercussions. This issue spans all parties and affects all branches of government, to varying degrees.

The detrimental impact of privatisation in Australia must be addressed. Forty years of neoliberalism have significantly weakened one of the world's finest social systems. Our health system is burdened by excessive public administration and rampant private profiteering. In education, inner-city private schools receive far more funding than necessary, while public schools struggle for resources. Universities see their graduates burdened with unjust debts due to the punitive HECS and HELP schemes, leaving many unable to find suitable employment. Instead of treating these essential services as investments, they are regarded as commodities accessible only to the wealthy, serving as barriers that exclude the less privileged. A healthy, educated population is crucial for a modern Australia.

Reform has been made difficult due to highly concentrated media ownership in Australia, where very wealthy right-wing men control the media. While independent media does an excellent job of holding major players accountable, its impact is limited. Successive governments have entrenched rather than curtailed media power, even to their own disadvantage. There are credible arguments suggesting that at least three of the four major companies are run by individuals unfit to hold a license under the law. Until Australia finds the courage to curtail or even dismantle the current system, real reform will remain challenging, if not impossible. The public depends on high-quality journalism to stay informed about government actions, both positive and negative. However, the current system often fails to inform the public adequately, instead acting as a protection racket for certain members of Parliament, creating divisions and distractions from serious issues, or showing bias towards right-wing parties. This is an untenable situation for a modern, informed, and engaged nation.

Australia is a nation that has not quite reached its potential consistently. With a bit of leadership, courage, and vision, Australians could look forward to a prosperous, comfortable, and exciting future. We have outlined some of the issues in this book, and we can only hope that governments start working toward positive reform sooner rather than later. Advance Australia Fair, *indeed.*

*

DIVIDED OPINIONS

THE NEW POLITICS ANALYSIS OF THE 2019 YEAR IN AUSTRALIAN POLITICS

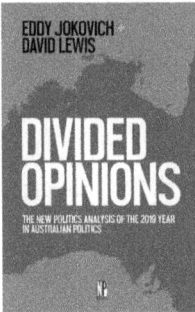

POLITICS, PROTEST, PANDEMIC

THE YEAR THAT CHANGED AUSTRALIA

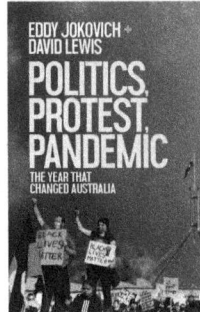

As the mainstream media struggles to retain audiences and survive under new business models and shrinking revenue streams, independents are filling in the gaps left behind by the older mastheads. New Politics is one of the more important voices appearing in this new landscape, and *Divided Opinions* presents some of the best work from the monthly podcast, and a selection of articles published during 2019. Guaranteed to make you think; aggravate, or inform and enlighten—and maybe all at once—this is a must-read analysis of one of the most dynamic years ever in Australian politics.

Available in paperback and ebook.

Divided Opinions: The New Politics analysis of the 2019 year in Australian politics
ISBN: 978-0-6481644-5-6
ISBN (Amazon): 978-1-6611355-7-7
338 pages

2020 was one of the most dramatic years in human history, shaped by the coronavirus pandemic that influenced society in so many different ways, combining health, politics, economics, business and education into the one sphere—and that proved to be difficult for many governments around the world to manage. *Politics, Protest, Pandemic: The year that changed Australia* is the story of the year in Australian federal politics, told through a collection of extended political essays from the New Politics Australia podcast series. This is a must-read analysis of one of the most dynamic years ever in Australian political history.

Available in paperback and ebook.

Politics, Protest, Pandemic: The year that changed Australia
ISBN: 978-0-6481644-8-7
ISBN (Amazon): 979-8-7372030-8-5
414 pages

DIARY OF AN ELECTION VICTORY

LABOR'S RISE TO POWER

In early 2020 at the onset of the coronavirus pandemic, Morrison held record high electoral ratings and Albanese was told to not worry about the next election: it was already out of reach and best to focus on the 2025 election and beyond. In 2022, Labor saw an opportunity: Morrison had made promises he ultimately couldn't deliver and it unravelled quickly. *Diary of An Election Victory* explores the key political moments of the 2022 election year, Morrison's demise, and Albanese's ascendancy and victory against the odds. It's a must-read analysis of one of the most dynamic and unusual election results ever in Australia's political history.

Available in paperback and ebook.

Diary of an Election Victory:
ISBN (paperback):   978-0-6456392-1-6
ISBN (hardback):   978-0-6456392-2-3
ISBN (Amazon):   979-8-3681569-7-2
304 pages

RISING PHOENIX, FALLING SHADOWS

THE YEAR IN AUSTRALIAN POLITICS

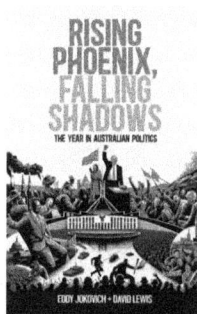

This exploration of Australia's political landscape in 2023 uncovers a year that began with high hopes, yet was marred by a series of unmet expectations and enduring challenges: the Voice to Parliament referendum and its subsequent defeat, the persistent housing crisis, cost of living and environmental concerns, AUKUS and Palestine—guiding the reader through the intricate web of political and social dynamics that define contemporary Australia. *Rising Phoenix, Falling Shadows* is a compelling read for anyone interested in understanding the multifaceted nature of governance and public policy in Australia.

Available in paperback and ebook.

Rising Phoenix, Falling Shadows: The year in Australian politics
ISBN (paperback):   978-0-6456392-9-2
ISBN (Amazon):   979-8-8720426-0-0
446 pages

ABOUT THE EDITORS

EDDY JOKOVICH is editor of *New Politics*, and co-presenter of the New Politics Australia podcast. He has worked as a journalist, publisher, author, political analyst, campaigner, war correspondent, and lecturer in media studies at the University of Technology, Sydney and the University of Sydney; has a wide range of experience working in editorial and media production work and is Director of ARMEDIA, a publishing and communications company specialising in public interest media.

DAVID LEWIS is co-presenter of the New Politics Australia podcast, historian, musicologist, musician and political scientist based in Sydney. His lecturing and research interests include roots music, popular music, Australian, UK and US politics and crime fiction. He has published in *Music Forum Australia*, *Eureka Street*, *Quadrant*, *Crikey* and has edited several books.

NEW POLITICS AUSTRALIA is a weekly podcast, providing analysis and opinions on Australia politics. It can be found at Apple podcasts, Amazon Audible and Spotify, and many other online providers.

www.ingramcontent.com/pod-product-compliance
Lightning Source LLC
Chambersburg PA
CBHW051721020426
42333CB00014B/1093